Best wishes,
Helga H...

"DON'T WORRY ABOUT A THING, DEAR"

Why Women Need Financial Intimacy

✳ ✳ ✳

By
Helga Hayse

Copyright ©2006 by Helga Hayse
All rights reserved.

Published by Primelife Publishing
San Mateo, CA 94402

Printed in the United States of America

ISBN 0-9778368-2-7 Print Edition

Library of Congress Control Number: 2006901820

Publisher's note

This publication is intended to provide accurate information about the subject matter covered. The information should be used as a general guide and not as a legal or financial blueprint for action. Readers are urged to seek personal legal or financial advice before taking any steps towards formal estate planning.

The publisher is not engaged in providing financial, legal or other professional services with regard to the subject matter. If financial or legal advice is desired or required, the service of a qualified professional person should be sought.

With the exception of the author, names and significant details about persons in this book have been changed to protect their privacy.

Original Cover Art: Edward Sorel,
The New Yorker Magazine, October 4, 1993

Cover/Book Design: Bruce Marion Studios

Acknowledgments

My daughters taught me most of what I learned about myself in the years since my husband died. To Emily, thank you for helping me, always with love, to pierce my protective fictions; to Julie, for your unconditional presence and love; to Linda, for encouraging me to stay with the writing even when the muse didn't show up.

I am grateful to friends who helped me rebuild my life and who sustain me still. Ardy Bazarian, Jim Charnes, Sue Gilbert, Deb and Stan Jernigan, Sydney Kapchan, Julia Michael, Sally Pera, Sherri Rose, Ellen Schwab, Steve Tulkin and Lisa Wolfklain. How would I have endured without you?

For special insights and inspiration, thanks also to Marya Alexander and Joni Arredia. You mentored and inspired me from afar. To Cliff Pletschet, thank you for my first media break when I launched the seminars in 2001; and to Shev Rush, my editor, who 'got it' from the start and can't wait for his mother, and her friends, to 'get it', too.

To the seminar participants who shared with me how they used the information to change their relationships and to the women who confided their concerns in very candid interviews - thank you for trusting me.

Special heartfelt thanks to Edward Sorel, whose illustration for The New Yorker Magazine cover on October 4, 1993, captured through art what I am trying to say in print. I am honored by the privilege of sharing it with others. The first exploration of concepts and action described in this book was at a meeting of 15 women on October 4, 1993. I've kept the cover all these years to remind me of how far I've come.

Finally, thank you to The New Yorker Magazine for permission to use the cover.

TABLE of CONTENTS

Part One: It's Personal

Part Two: It's Not Personal

Part Three: Getting Intimate About Money

Part Four: Practicing Safe Marriage

Appendix

Part One

It's Personal

Chapter One

***

Why I Wrote This Book

"When patterns are broken, new worlds emerge."

Tuli Kupferberg

I loved my husband and suffered agonizing trauma and loss after he died suddenly in an accident. But after the early years of sharp grief subsided and I began to pick up the pieces of my life, I started to think of him as a more idealized version of the man I married than as the man he actually was. After many false starts writing this book with that idealized image in mind, I realized I hadn't been emotionally honest with others, or myself, about the relief I felt to be free of the financial pressures -- and resentments -- I often experienced in our marriage.

These years of being on my own have allowed me to live life without the distorting filter of my husband's preferences and dreams. But without the financial preparation I completed -- some on my own, some with my husband -- my life would have been dramatically different. I would never have recovered financially from the burden of his death. I would never have forgiven him for risking my future safety to achieve his dreams. And I might have felt guilty forever for all the things I hadn't shared with him.

Today, I would never allow someone to make financial decisions for me without discussing the consequences of those actions first. I would insist on understanding anything I sign – a contract, an income tax return, a letter of intent -- that would obligate me financially. But I wasn't like that during my two marriages. The first ended in divorce; the second ended in death.

Like so many other women I know, my marriage had a public face and a private face. It endured because of protective fictions on my part that ate away at me slowly, but steadily. I realize now how those fictions enabled the relationship to function.

Writing this book has given me a profound sense of responsibility about encouraging women to assert themselves in changing the status quo in their relationship. It takes courage to move past one's fear and break the pattern. The concern about loss is real. What lies on the other side of action is often an unknown.

However, financial intimacy is not about trust. It's about participation and being a well-informed equal partner. It's about knowledge and joint decisions, mutual respect and self-esteem. It's about protection for you in case something doesn't work out in the marriage. In other words, those characteristics are, or should be, the cornerstones of a loving marriage.

My personal story is a backdrop against which to frame a larger and more widespread problem that exists for millions of women in the United States: the lack of understanding and participation in marital finances. Our willingness to let our husband handle the finances in the marriage impacts our own financial safety and our ability to cope in the event of widowhood or divorce.

That's just what I did. I assumed that my husband was smarter about money than I was and that he had my best interests at heart. In retrospect, it's clear that he was doing what he wanted to do – build his business, hope it would be successful, and, in that way, serve both our interests. What he failed to do, and what I didn't know I should do until my own realization about financial intimacy, was build in the protections for me if things didn't go according to plan. As it so happened, nothing went according to plan.

I'm not unique. Like many of you, I confused money with love and didn't understand that the institution of marriage removes your financial autonomy. Whatever else it may mean emotionally, a marriage license is first and foremost a contract of partnership recognized by the state as a legally binding agreement. Once you say, "I Do", you are one-half of a legal and financial entity. From that point on, whatever your husband is doing, or intends to do financially, whether you know about it or not, you are, or will be, doing it, too. The same holds true for your husband. But if he is the one who is controlling your marital finances, you are the one at risk. You're the one for whom I'm writing this book.

Oddly enough, in most states, it's easier to get married than it is to buy a gun or get a driver's license. For the gun, you must wait 10 days, or whatever the law is in your state, while the authorities run identity checks on you. A 16-year-old can get a driver's license after passing a written and driving test. The authorities can revoke either the permit for the gun or the driver's license if you engage in illegal behavior.

In my county in California, you can get married within 30 minutes of applying for a marriage license. What does it take? Bride and groom have to be there, show an official ID such as a driver's license or a passport, and pay $78 (cash only) for the license. No blood test is required. No questions asked. No skills evaluated. No competency demonstrated. No background check instigated. In other words, the state makes it appallingly easy to get married – and miserably complicated to work your way through the financial consequences of widowhood or divorce.

That's why money – understanding it and being able to talk about it in a conscious, responsible and respectful way – is as important to your marriage as sex, romance and love. We lavish our attention on the latter three – and assume that money will just take care of itself. It doesn't.

The sad truth is that going into marriage, it's all about love. Coming out of it, either through widowhood or divorce, it's all about money.

In this book, I'm not going to give you detailed or complicated legal or financial advice. My goal is to alert you to your rights in marriage and how those rights are compromised by romantic fictions about marriage. I hope that after reading through the chapters, you will seek expert legal and financial advice for the actions you need to take to protect you if something happens to end your marriage.

Chapter Two

* * *

My Wake-Up Call

"Life is what happens while you're
busy making other plans."

John Lennon

I t happened by accident. I was looking for a new
car and answered an ad for a low mileage
Cadillac for $5,000. The seller was a woman
who lived in my neighborhood. She suggested I
stop by her house. The navy blue car was parked
in the driveway. When she answered the doorbell,
I noticed briefly that she looked like me – same
height, hair color, and age. I introduced myself, and
we went to look at the car, which seemed to be in
perfect condition. She told me to feel free to have
my own mechanic check it. I said, "Great. It's a
deal."

Suddenly, her eyes filled with tears. I asked her
if she was okay, instinctively reaching out to touch
her arm. She told me she'd been widowed a few
months earlier and that the car she was selling to

me was a gift from her husband. While it was fully paid for, she had to raise money to pay off the lease on her late husband's car. Other bills were mounting, her husband's will was tied up in probate, and her children were bickering about who would get what.

"I am so angry at him for dying," she said, tears rolling down her cheeks. "I'm angry at myself for not paying more attention to our finances. I don't know where to begin. I don't want my children to handle financial things for me. I'll never forgive him for leaving me in such a mess."

That was my epiphany, my moment of sharp clarity about my own life -- my 'Oprah moment', if you will. While strongly feeling compassion for this widow's grief and loss, I vividly and clearly saw that I would be in the same situation as she was if my husband died. Like her, I had ceded control of marital finances. I recognized in myself many of the frustrations and feelings of helplessness that she was sharing with me.

I often felt these same feelings over the sixteen years we were married, but ignored them. I had the illusion of safety because I was married to a man I loved. I handled the financial details for my own business, but at home, my husband was running the financial show. This way of thinking is inconceivable to me now, but it felt completely natural then.

My husband was an entrepreneur with a growing company and a continuing need for business credit. Whenever he brought home bank papers for yet another business loan and said, "Sign here Honey", I would sign. Occasionally, I'd worry about what I was signing, but he'd reassure me with his usual optimistic "Don't worry honey, it will all be fine" – seductive, dangerous words for women not involved in their marital finances.

Such is the power of love that we soothe ourselves with the myth that it conquers all. Throughout these years, I doubt that my husband deliberately lied or concealed things from me. I trusted his personal ethics and integrity. Time and again, I squelched the feelings of vulnerability I had given all the debt we were carrying. I didn't know exactly how much it was, but from the way we lived, I knew it must be a lot. I told myself that he knew what he was doing, that he loved me and that he would never deliberately put us in financial danger.

Some people have a higher tolerance for risk than others. My husband's and my money styles and ambition levels were different. His dreams were more expensive than mine. His dream of building a successful manufacturing business required heavy investment in equipment and personnel. My dream was to be a successful consultant to businesses who worked with seniors. No equipment, no real estate, no payroll.

My husband was entirely focused on the future. For example, around our house, he'd plant acorns, knowing that in 20 years, there would be oak trees. I preferred annuals and perennials, knowing that I'd enjoy color and bloom this year and maybe next. Somewhere along the line, I made his dreams more important than mine. And I didn't know how to turn that around.

It was bizarre: I loved my husband, but I was scared to death about our financial situation and didn't know what I could do about it. All those years, I thought stress naturally went along with being married to an entrepreneur. I didn't connect the dots because I didn't realize how dangerous it could be.

Standing in the woman's driveway that sunny morning and listening to her story brought my own feelings of vulnerability sharply to the surface. I worried how I would cope if my husband died. I wondered how many women were in similar situations of letting their husbands handle the marital finances and trusting that all would be well.

Because my background is journalism and I work as a professional writer, I decided to research the subject for myself. I learned that I wasn't alone in not participating in my marital finances. It was widespread and, in community property states, especially dangerous for wives.

At first, I gathered information intending to write an article about it. I asked widows I knew if they would talk with me and if they could connect me with other widows. I asked my married friends if they were willing to be interviewed. Eventually, this network allowed me to conduct over one hundred interviews. One after another, women told me stories that confirmed my worst fears: married women unaware of their finances are at considerable risk financially. In community property states, the risk is even greater.

I also interviewed husbands, including my own. I learned that men resist thinking about their own mortality. Estate planning, life insurance, wills, vulnerability, unpredictability – subjects relating to death - are topics men don't like to think or talk about.

Three things came up repeatedly in my interviews with men. First, a fear that if they plan, and once all the papers are signed, they will die.

Superstition to be sure, but powerful nevertheless.

The second thing was procrastination: "I'm going to do it. I just don't want anyone to nag me about it." They seemed to think if they ignored the subject, it would just go away.

The third thing was a belief that their wife would be fine. "She's educated, she's smart -- she can always get a job. Besides, the kids will help her."

What would happen to our own financial interest if something were to happen to our husbands was taboo. If men don't like to talk about death, and women are uncomfortable talking about money, no planning will take place. If we're not involved in the finances, how are we supposed to prepare for what we know can happen?

I shared with my husband some of what I had learned from my research:

- Wives outlive their husbands by 8-10 years.

- One of six women over 40 is widowed.

- The average age of widows in the U.S. is 56 years old.

- Most widows suffer a loss of income and a severe change in lifestyle.

- Most are unprepared to cope on their own.

- There are four widows for every widower.

- Husbands lose less financially if their wife dies before them.

I pointed out to my husband that my signature was right next to his on every company contract and loan document. His son, who worked at the company and wanted to run it after my husband retired, had no financial obligation for the debts incurred by the company. His house wasn't pledged as collateral against the credit line. Creditors could never come after him if something happened to his father. His signature wasn't on any of the bank paperwork. His wife and children would not be impacted if the company folded. He slept peacefully, knowing that his dad was doing what it took to keep the company going. And if that meant that his stepmother was taking one more risk, signing on one more credit line, who cared?

There was more, but my husband got the idea. He was surprised at my sense of urgency and knew this wasn't going to go away for me. He agreed to start the planning process.

Our discussions didn't always go smoothly. Some days we were angry with each other as things arose that we didn't want to face. He was openly irritated that he had to spend money on attorney's fees to do something he didn't want to do, which was think about his own death.

We disagreed on many things. For example, we both had children from a previous marriage. Whose children would get what proportion of the assets? Would the company have to be sold to keep me out of debt? How would we evaluate my contribution to the company's bottom line?

One by one, we tackled the hot buttons and the many questions we needed to address so that our planning would be comprehensive. Most important from my point of view was how I would be protected in case something happened to my husband.

What I learned through all this discussion was the truth about our financial life. All those tax returns I hadn't looked at, those contracts I had signed, those credit lines secured by my signature came crashing back into my mind at once, and I felt like a fly caught in a spider's web. It appeared that I was not in financial control of anything in my life.

———————————————

Looking back, I don't recall a premonition about anything bad happening to my husband. I just felt a sense of urgency that we take care of the planning now. I wanted my feelings acknowledged. I didn't want to be reassured that everything would be fine and lulled into a false sense of security. At that point, I had learned a lot about all the things that can and do go wrong when you're least expecting them.

Throughout this process, I continued with my research and interviews. Friends encouraged me to pull the information together and create a seminar on how women could protect themselves by learning about and participating in their marital finances. I began testing seminars locally. Many women shared how grateful they were for learning how to express concerns that we all share, but are too often unable to put into words. My purpose was not to provide financial or legal advice, but to teach women what I had learned, which was how important it is for us to participate, understand and plan for the unexpected.

In one of those strange twists of fate, a few weeks after the papers were signed, my husband returned from a week on the road visiting clients. I was away with a client who had an out-of-town event.

Sleep-deprived and fatigued, my husband poured a glass of wine and eased his body into the hot tub to relax in the comforting heat as we often did together when I was at home. The warm waters lulled him into a deep sleep.

When I returned the next day, I noticed that all the lights were on in the house. My black lab circled around me, signaling to me as he usually did when he was hungry. My heart skipped a few beats as I called out my husband's name. Why were all the lights on?

I moved through the house into the bedroom, but couldn't find my husband. I stepped outside the bedroom door onto the patio. There in the hot tub, my husband's body lay immobilized in the steamy soft bubbles of the jets. The new thermostat he had installed just the week before had maintained the hot tub temperature at a steady 105 degrees.

I screamed and raced for the phone to call 911. The operator tried to calm me down, asking me to feel for a pulse in his neck. I couldn't touch him. The body in the hot tub was discolored and shriveled. I remember screaming, "Do something, somebody do something!" I must finally have been able to give my address to her because, within moments, I could hear sirens as sheriff's cars were dispatched. They were headed for my home.

To this day, I recoil at the sound of sirens. My ears still echo with the hoarseness of my screams and the words of the sheriff as he gently pried me loose from the side of tub and guided me back into the house.

That morning, I began my journey from wife to widow. I became one of 12 million widows in the U.S. It would take five years before I felt able to once again lead the seminars

The timing and irony of his death stunned my family and me. My daughters asked me what they should do because they knew I dealt with the subject in the seminar. I went to my computer, printed out two pages of the seminar resource book, took two sleeping pills and went to bed. Ironically, I had become the test subject for the effectiveness of what I teach other women.

Nothing I had researched could prepare me for the trauma and tragedy of my husband's death. But the practical information I had gathered and the financial planning we completed before he died eased some of my financial burden.

Ultimately, I'd have to say it was just dumb luck that all the papers were signed before my husband died. Had he died one month earlier, our paper-work would've been incomplete and my situation as desperate as if there had been no planning at all. Unsigned drafts don't count as legal documents.

Part Two

It's Not Personal

Chapter Three

✳ ✳ ✳

Redefining Intimacy

"Intimacy is what makes a marriage,
not a ceremony, not a piece of
paper from the state."

Kathleen Norris

I believe we need a wider definition of intimacy, a concept we currently link with the physical, sexual or emotional revealing of ourself to another person in a most private way. We may have been intimate with many people in all or some of these ways before we married. However, marriage takes intimacy to another level because we commit to a shared future with another person, expecting that the intimacy we engage in will be reciprocated.

Unfortunately, marital finances (one of the most important areas of intimacy) are often ignored, taken for granted, or viewed as a potential minefield, and thus, an area to be avoided. Or, as Jenny, one of the women I interviewed for this book, said, "I go along to get along." You can be sure that Jenny is experiencing difficulty in other areas of intimacy in her marriage as well.

As I researched the concept of intimacy, I noticed a strange and almost opposite meaning of the word compared to the way we usually think of it. Intimacy is also linked with secrecy, as in privacy and confidentiality. Typically, this kind of intimacy is not reciprocal.

For example, my gynecologist knows my body in a more intimate way than I know hers. Similarly, my accountant knows everything about my finances – and I know nothing about his. My therapist knows my most intimate thoughts without my having a clue about anything in her life. I don't expect to have a continuing personal relationship beyond the scope of the service they provide, and I am not at risk if I don't know them the way they know me. However, secrecy, or keeping financial matters private, can be as deadly to a marriage as infidelity. It erodes trust and devalues a couple's commitment to a lasting and loving partnership.

Unfortunately, full financial disclosure is still treated as taboo in many marriages, especially when the man makes the big money decisions. A wife may be contributing a significant amount of money through her work, yet may go decades knowing little about her shared finances. In many instances, her financial insecurity does not become evident until she is widowed or divorced, the worst possible times to begin grappling with money troubles or decisions or learning about the basics of money management.

The problem goes deeper than that. Failure to achieve financial intimacy in your marriage creates a climate of resentment, suspicion and lack of trust. If you're feeling angry, patronized, ignored or shut out when it comes to finances, your feelings are certain to spill over into other areas of the marriage. Sex, honesty, closeness, trust, parenting – all will be affected on a conscious or subconscious level. Bad feelings don't go away; they redistribute. One woman I interviewed said it very colorfully: "He expects oral sex twice a night, but he won't tell me what our net worth is."

In a sense, one could argue that intimacy is the opposite of romance. Intimacy allows a deeper, closer understanding of another person or situation based on revealing what actually exists. Romance, on the other hand, seeks to create a quality or environment that is remote from everyday life. (We will look more closely at romance and how it affects marriage in a later chapter.)

Let's get back to my accountant. Although the flow of intimacy is one-dimensional because I know nothing about his finances, it doesn't matter. What he does with his money won't affect me personally. But if I engage in romantic illusion about my finances, thinking that everything will be all right because I want it to be, he will point out to me the consequences of my romantic thinking.

The fact is, financial intimacy creates financial transparency between husband and wife. It's not about trusting, hoping or assuming that your husband is doing everything right. It's about knowing and understanding what he is doing because everything he does affects you. That's what being an equal partner means. You are part of a fifty/fifty relationship. In fact, it has nearly the same structural characteristics of a business partnership. (We'll also explore that concept later in this book.)

As a partner, you have a right, and the law supports your right, to all the financial information about your partnership. If you are the primary breadwinner in your family, your husband has that same right. You are not entitled to special treatment because you are a woman, but to equal treatment because you are a partner. You may earn less than your husband, but you take the same amount of financial risk for decisions made within your partnership.

As you read through this book, I hope to demystify many of the things we take for granted in marriage. After we've explored the subject, and when you're ready to discuss your thoughts with your husband, you may be pleasantly surprised to find that your husband responds enthusiastically. You may learn that he is concerned that you'll be at a disadvantage if something happens to him. The point is, if you don't ask, you won't know what you need to know if something does happen to him or you do find yourself faced with a divorce situation.

On the other hand, your husband may not want you to participate for a variety of reasons, including control, leverage, jealousy, fear, distrust or a sincere belief that you can't be trusted with financial information.

Remember this: his reasons don't matter. If he's not sharing information with you, he's not being a responsible partner. If you're not asking, you're not being a responsible partner, either. And worse yet, you may be doing what I did, using protective fictions to say it doesn't matter.

If you find yourself widowed or divorced, some things will be immediately clear. You will need financial resources and the skills to manage them. You will need to understand basic finances so you won't have to rely on family members, friends or a financial advisor to tell you what to do. You will need to understand and sign contracts on your own. You will need to know how to do the financial things that you relied on your husband to do for you.

However, if you were financially intimate during your marriage, you will be able to do all these things.

It was surprising for me to learn during interviews and from my research that many boomer-age women follow the traditional marriage model at home and cede responsibility for marital finances to their husband, even if they work and are accustomed to making financial decisions in their jobs or businesses.

After nearly five decades of feminism, many of us still have trouble separating the truths and myths that co-exist in marriage. Truths often make us uncomfortable; myths appeal to our deepest needs as women. We grow up with fairy tales and romance fantasies perpetuated in the media, which often creates the unconscious desire to be taken care of by the man we love. I plead guilty on both counts – I ignored the truths and lived by many of the myths in my own two marriages.

Widowhood happens to millions of women. The difference for me was that I had the information I needed to start a dialogue with my husband before he died. If we had not done any planning to protect me, or if the papers hadn't been signed in time, none of our efforts would have been legally binding. It would have been too late for taking the actions required to protect me from creditors. I would have owed more money than I could have repaid in two lifetimes.

If you handle the finances in your marriage, you're probably fine, but you will benefit from the emotional information in the pages that follow. Hopefully, you and your husband already have an estate plan in place with all the papers signed.

If you're engaged to be married, you must go in with your eyes open. Taking the lessons from this book and applying them at the outset of your marriage will go a long way to making sure your impending marriage is successful in the long-term.

If you're widowed or divorced, you may already be going through some of the scenarios I've described and need help now. Or, you may remarry and once again be at financial risk down the road. Preparing now for any eventuality is a smart move, and this book will help you make that move.

Chapter Four

***

The Big Picture

"Other men die; but I am not an other;
therefore, I'll not die."

Vladimir Nabakov

A t first glance, nothing seems more impersonal than statistics, yet statistics give us a
look at the big picture. Each of us fits into
some demographic profile tracked by the federal
and state census agencies. These agencies don't
know our names or care if we're happily married or
not. We're just numbers being crunched in a
computer.

On the following page, you'll see how some of
those numbers look when it comes to women.

Some Facts of Life

- Being widowed ranks highest on the Stress Related Disease Scale.

- Divorce ranks second on that list.

- One of two marriages ends in divorce.

- Every year in the U.S, there are about 2.3 million marriages.

- In the United States, there are 11,975,325 widows and 2,699,175 widowers.

- The ratio of widows to widowers is 4 to 1.

- The average age women are widowed is 56.

- One of six women over age 40 is widowed.

- Wives outlive husbands by 8-10 years if they marry at the same age.

- Average longevity for women is 80 years old.

- Average longevity for men is 74 years old.

- 85 out of 100 women will be alone sometime in their life.

- Husbands have less to lose financially if their wife dies.

- 80 percent of life insurance money is used up during the first year of widowhood.

- Widowers and divorced men remarry younger women.

- Widows are poorer than married women of the same age.

- Most wives are financially unprepared for widowhood.

Sources: University of Washington State Medical School / 2000 U.S. Census

A cartoon in the New Yorker shows a man seated in his underwear on a doctor's examining table. The doctor is standing near him. The caption reads "Tell me the truth Doc, how long do I have to ignore these symptoms?"

According to the Greek physician Hippocrates, a wise man ought to realize that his health is his most valuable possession. Unfortunately, most men fail to take this advice seriously.

Statistics show that your husband will probably die before you. Since the average age at which women are widowed is 56, with the average longevity age at 83, it's likely you'll be spending over two decades on your own whether you want to or not. In fact, there's a high probability that you will, if only because the men who might be available as mates are often marrying or living with younger women.

Why do women live longer? Researchers believe a number of factors are involved, including protective hormones, emotionally-supportive friends, preventive medical checkups, better cooperation with doctors' advice, and greater ability to adapt to life's changes, to name just a few.

Your husband may love you dearly, yet be totally resistant to changing his behavior just because you want him to. You may think, "What's so complicated about stopping smoking, or drinking, or getting annual checkups, losing weight, or exercising more?" You may think, "If he really loves me, he'd do it." But, you'd be wrong. That's wishful thinking. The truth is that we have no control over someone else's behavior, whether they love us or we love them, or whether they are men or women.

It's an illusion to think we can change someone else's behavior. Your husband won't change unless he decides it's important to him. That's a problem when it comes to being one-half of a partnership. In this legal and financial partnership called marriage, your partner's behavior directly affects you. Bad health habits affect you. Physical risk-taking affects you. Financial decisions affect you. Once you sign that marriage license, you may be a wife, but you've also entered the arena as a business partner. Consider Sandra's story:

"When Burt and I married, I was 32, he was 35. We met at the ad agency where we both worked. Shortly after we married, Burt and a friend formed a printing company, which had been a dream of his for a long time. We postponed our honeymoon until we felt our finances could handle it better. After working hard for two years, we took a week off and went skiing in Aspen. On the last day of our vacation, Burt was loading our skis on the rack of the car when he grabbed his chest. A moment later, he collapsed at my feet. By the time the paramedics arrived, Burt was dead of a heart attack.

Burt had no life insurance and no will. The company he had formed with his partner, a 50-50 partnership, had recently ordered expensive press equipment. His partner was involved in the sales and marketing end of the business. Burt handled the money; both partners co-signed all business documents. Burt's partner decided not to continue in the business on his own.

It took me four years to pay off the business debts

we had incurred. No one let me off the hook because I was a widow. No one cared that I wasn't involved in the business. Burt's business partner was very matter-of-fact about how to split the obligation. I felt like the whole marriage had been reduced to an ordinary business transaction."

Chapter Five

* * *

Why People Don't Plan

"Man plans and God laughs."

An Old Jewish Proverb

I n this chapter, we are going to discuss some ways in which we convince ourselves that it's all right not to plan. We'll start with impersonality, but will move on to denial, "benefliction", fear of dying, superstition, and optimism.

We don't like to think about the impersonality of the universe. That's why many of us pray and have faith that our prayers will be answered.

But seen in a context outside of faith, destiny is really an impersonal numbers game. Prepared or not, the odds are the same. Something either will happen or it won't. Cancer happens. Accidents occur. Planes crash. We lose people we love. Most of the time, we have no control, even though we like to think we do.

Acknowledging that things just happen means that everything is random. And a random universe is frightening. It makes us feel invisible, unimportant and vulnerable. It's comforting to think that we can exert some leverage or control over our fate based on our actions. But, the only thing in our control is to protect ourselves against the things not in our control. So, why don't more people plan?

On an African safari a few years ago, our group visited a Masai village. We noticed that the women in the village had a gap in their lower front teeth. Our guide explained that their teeth are deliberately knocked out because tetanus is a recurring problem. The gap in the lower teeth allows nursing mothers who may develop tetanus to sustain themselves with the tribe's nourishing drink of goat's milk and blood.

The obvious solution is to eliminate tetanus. But tetanus shots are not generally available in the Masai Mara. I couldn't help thinking that this simple act of knocking out two bottom teeth so that nourishment could be sipped through a straw was a model of good planning.

We behave in ways we think are safe because we want to be safe. According to Daniel Goleman, author of *Vital Lies, Simple Truths: The Psychology of Self-Deception*, we learn the tactics of self deception very early. "We need those protective fictions and blind spots to allow our relationships to function, balancing what is lacking in the relationship or the environment and closing that gap by what we create," he writes.

In other words, we see what we look for and not what we look at. Protective fictions are useful for getting some of our relationship needs met, but the price can be high. These enabling fictions are a Faustian bargain at best.

Gina was in a second marriage. Her husband urged her to let his investment advisor also manage her money. When her husband died unexpectedly, Gina learned that he had set up a trust that included the money she had received in her divorce settlement from her first marriage:

"The financial advisor had combined our money. The life insurance my husband took out to protect me was also designated to go into the trust. I would receive income from the trust, but the financial advisor would decide how to invest the principal, including the money I had originally brought to the marriage. The principal would be divided between me and his children from his first marriage. I would have to challenge the trust in court if I was to free up my own money. I never realized he had set things up this way. To be honest, I was always uncomfortable that he kept all our records. But I didn't want him to think I didn't trust him. I also didn't want him to think I had married him for his money."

The price of silence on an important issue like marital finances, where husband and wife are equally responsible, can be physically stressful, financially dangerous and ultimately demeaning. If you don't know and don't want to know about your marital finances, you are signaling to your husband that he alone is in charge.

A division of labor, where he handles the financial matters, is one thing. Being in charge is another. If you're not participating in the finances, you should at least be current and informed on a regular basis across the board about the finances.

Unfortunately, even when women decide they want to be involved, it may take some time before they can comfortably speak up about it. Here is what Sally, a woman I interviewed for this book, had to say:

"Just knowing that I need to do things differently isn't enough for me. I need time to process. I feel my whole life will change, even if I want that change. It's scary for me to allow the feelings to surface. I'll know I should be doing something differently, but I can't act immediately when I get these feelings. It goes against everything I was raised to be – a good girl, a helpmate, loyal, and compromising. Even when I realized how dependent I was on my husband, I couldn't allow myself to attend your seminar. With all the tools and information about communication, it still took me months to break my pattern and speak up."

A New Yorker cartoon shows a couple strolling arm in arm. She is saying to him, "You never tell me anything. Keep up the good work."

The ostrich is a seven-foot, gawky bird, with hooded eyelids and seductively fluttering eyelashes, and a brain that is smaller than its eye. When it senses danger, it lays its neck flat on the ground, closes its eyes and buries its head in the grass, dirt, sand or wherever it finds itself. It feels safe even though its rump is still high in the air. We laugh at the silliness of this behavior. We even have a name for it, "the ostrich syndrome," which refers to our ignoring something that's obvious.

There are many reasons that people don't plan. One of the most-common reasons people don't plan is denial. This is a way in which we censor ourselves before thoughts or feelings can surface. Unlike the ostrich syndrome, where we think we're safe if we don't think about something, denial is a state of mind we don't even know we're in. The ostrich may be guilty of faulty reasoning, but it is not in denial.

Denial is the refusal to accept things as they are. It can be a powerful antidote to anxiety, but does little to change the source of that anxiety.

Mardi Horowitz, a psychiatrist, writes in her book *The Denial of Stress* that there are many forms of denial: "We realign the facts to obscure what is really going on. It's useful because we repress what we fear. The world seems normal and we're not particularly bothered by what we don't know."

Just as fish who don't know they swim in water until the water is removed, we are in danger of nasty surprises if we don't know what our financial picture really is. For instance, here's what Sarah, another interviewee, had to say:

"I just assumed that money from his pension would be part of what we'd live on in retirement. But when my husband died, I learned that his first wife would be getting half of his pension benefits because that was negotiated as part of their divorce settlement. He never told me that; I never thought to ask about it. "

———————————

The term 'benefliction' was coined by Dr. Harry

Berger, Professor of Literature at UC Santa Cruz. He used the word in conjunction with teaching King Lear. Another name for this syndrome is 'learned helplessness', described by Dr. Martin Seligman in his studies of depression. He observed peoples' perceptions of helplessness and their responses to those perceptions in situations where they believe they have no choice.

Benefliction is a condescending behavior designed to keep people from asserting themselves. The word isn't found in a dictionary, but I believe it should be. The behavior is operative when parents are overprotective or anticipate their child's every need, thus keeping the child from developing the resources to deal with delay, frustration and challenge.

Benefliction combines the good ('bene') with the bad ('fliction'), as when a wife asks her husband about their finances and he says "Don't worry about a thing, dear." That's benefliction.

"I've taken care of everything" is another phrase that makes it awkward for a woman to press on for more information. Often, the next request for information is answered by "Don't you trust me?" Benefliction is condescending and patronizing. It cuts off further communication about the subject. Whatever her reason, a wife who asks for more information about marital finances should get it, without a dismissive and disabling response.

So why don't people do the one thing that works to protect them against the things they can't control? Why don't they plan for death?

As a culture, we avoid talking about death. We have euphemisms for dying. People pass away or cross over. We act as if we, and those we love, are going to live forever. But we will die. We just don't know when. We need to recognize what facing it honestly can do for our life and for the life of the people we love. In fact, we have to think about it. Only then are we able to put it out of our minds.

Psychiatrists have long equated the reluctance to think about drawing-up a will with fear of death. Writing a will means having to admit one's mortality. It also means having to think about giving up control of one's assets. Say the word 'widow' to many men and you go straight to the heart of their own fears about death. With one word, you wipe out a husband's illusion of immortality.

My husband was a good example. He rarely thought about death. He was busy building his business. When he retired, he planned to remodel the house. And, of course, he would play tennis every day as he always had. Nothing would change. Didn't he always get a clean bill of health? And isn't it morbid to be talking about something that isn't going to happen for many years? Death was so far out on the horizon for him that he never thought about it. It wasn't part of his plan.

'Till death do us part' are words men say as part of the marriage ceremony. It's traditional and no one thinks much about it. It's a declaration that this woman he is marrying is his true love and will be forever. Men don't want to be reminded of their vulnerability. So how is a wife supposed to raise the subject of her fears and concerns of how she would cope on her own if she were widowed?

I remember reading a personals ad years ago that

said: "Confirmed bachelor changes mind. Ready for marriage and family. Good job, good habits, good values. Life insurance policy needs beneficiary."

I thought that this man must really get it. I hope he found the woman of his dreams. Purchasing life insurance is a tremendous act of love. It shows a commitment to the welfare of someone you love even though you will not be around to enjoy it with her.

Lily Pincus writes in *Death and the Family*: "Thinking and talking about death need not be morbid. It may be quite the opposite. Ignorance and fear of death overshadow life, while knowing about and accepting death erases this shadow and makes life freer of fears and anxieties."

We treat death with an awe and respect that ought to be reserved for life. Part of this stems from fear of the unknown and what may await us after we die. But since there's nothing we can do about that, our energies would be better spent on what awaits us after a traumatic change in our life, such as the death of a spouse.

One could almost say that being able to discuss death is a form of intimacy. We have no reason to discuss it with someone who isn't important in our life. Whether it's a husband or our children, the fact that we love them enough to trust them with our feelings and wishes about one of our deepest fears is a profound act of intimacy.

In youth, death seems remote. That alone should make it easier to discuss when a couple is young. As a couple ages, it becomes more difficult to initiate these important talks. Your husband has heard too much about women outliving men. He becomes defensive. He may even suspect that you might be trying to hurry him into the grave. Attempts at discussion of what will happen should you outlive him create tension and difficulties. Many women decide that it is better to trust him to do the right thing and to leave the matter unspoken. They're wrong. If you don't speak up, the financial consequences for you if he dies can be ruinous.

A child therapist told me, "Children of parents who are not afraid of death are not afraid of life". In that sense, education about death is education about life. I bought a grave so my children won't be faced with confusion about what Mom wanted. I showed them where it is, not far from where my home is. We joked about how nice the view is and that the tree near my piece of real estate is great for leaning against if they come to visit. Keeping it light means keeping it in perspective. It serves as an example for them, too, in how to discuss death with their own children.

When my mother heard bad news, she would rush for the salt shaker, turn on the gas stove and sprinkle salt for 30 seconds into the flame, certain that with this gesture, she was protecting herself against something bad happening to us. Some people carry a rabbit's foot or knock on wood when they say something good about their life.

Superstition is a powerful, if irrational and often subconscious, belief that keeps many men from taking action to protect their wife in case they die. It presumes a causal relationship between something we do or don't do and the outcome of some future event. The same thing happens when people refuse to talk about the possibility of death. Cynthia illustrates this with her story:

"We went through the whole process of estate planning. My husband signed all the financial papers, but is refusing to sign the durable powers of attorney for medical and financial decisions. He keeps saying he will. When I remind him that the papers aren't complete if he doesn't sign, he accuses me of nagging. His attorney calls, asking about the papers, and he tells him he's going to do it tomorrow, but he never does. He's convinced that, if all the papers aren't signed yet, he won't die. He knows it's not rational, but it makes him feel better. Even though I understand it, it's very frustrating for me."

If only we had that kind of power. If only we were the center of the universe, where what we do matters on a cosmic scale. It's comforting to think that a higher power is watching and rewarding or punishing, waiting until all the papers are in order and everything is signed before taking us away. It sounds so simple and silly, but this kind of thinking is real and widespread. Unfortunately, superstition impacts the lives of too many wives whose husbands won't follow through with the necessary arrangements to protect them. As Veronica told me:

"My husband's friend had a fatal heart attack on the tennis court the day after he and his wife signed their living trust. You try convincing my husband that the same won't happen to him."

Who would think that optimism, like longevity, has a downside? But it does.

Optimism is defined as expecting the best possible outcome. On the face of it, that sounds comforting and just what we want to hear when we are concerned about something. The problem with expecting the best possible outcome is that it ignores the odds. Toss a coin. But, the odds are always 50/50 for heads or tails, no matter how many times you throw the coin.

The odds of something bad happening are always 50 percent – they either will or they won't. Optimism is great, but unbridled optimism is just as bad as unbridled anything else. It ignores reality. We need our optimism to be tempered by realism, or what I call mature optimism.

Mature optimism recognizes that bad things can happen, things over which we have little or no control, and that it's not personal. It is not wishful or positive thinking. It is open and honest and recognizes the reality of things. It is practical and action oriented. It's based on analysis and the long view, with a good dose of hope thrown in.

Hope is terrific, a physical emotion that actually creates endorphins in our brain. Endorphins are the chemicals responsible for the runner's high and create the fuel for the gambler's winning streak. They give us the ability to keep doing what we're doing. While endorphins are great in the short run because we feel so good, in the long run, they keep us from taking corrective steps when we should.

Chapter Six

* * *

The Six Myths of Marriage

"The great enemy of truth is very
often not the lie – deliberate, contrived and
dishonest – but the myth – persistent,
persuasive and unrealistic."

John F. Kennedy

When I think of truth, I think of facts which can be seen, verified through experiment, or measured by dimension or weight. All other 'truths' are cultural; they are shared assumptions that we agree upon, based on our cultural background.

We modern women are still subject to the master myths from which the other 'truths' derive. It is a social construct which takes different forms in different cultures and evolves to reflect and serve the needs of each group. Marriage is not a natural process, nor is it subject to the laws of nature. There are no factual truths associated with marriage except one: when you marry, you become one legal and financial unit. And the only ways to legally end a modern marriage are through annulment, divorce or death.

Myths often masquerade as truths, making it hard to separate one from the other. From preliterate myths to the Bible, in fairy tales and tribal lore, through culture and customs, family and peer pressure, much of what we associate with marriage today is simply what we have repeated from generation to generation. Five decades of feminism didn't eliminate or measurably minimize our core desire to believe in fairy godmothers and other nurturing mythological stereotypes.

We modern women, raised with five decades of feminism, are still subject to the master myths from which the other 'truths' derive. The knight on the white horse rides through our imagination. We still want to believe that our marriage will be happy, that happily ever after can and will happen for us, that those to whom we willingly give power (and give power we do, whether we admit it or not) will make decisions in our best interests. I suggest that, once past childhood, it's naive to believe these fairy tales. It's especially dangerous to believe so in marriage.

Let's look at some of the myths that permeate our culture and our attitudes about marriage:

Myth 1:
Happy Marriages Start with a Great Wedding

There are 2.3 million marriages every year in the US, which is good news for the wedding industry. Each of those marriages represents proof of the triumph of romantic love and the endurance of traditional family structures. Of course, that statistic is balanced by another: one of two marriages end in divorce.

Every bride wants her wedding day to 'be perfect'. She may not be sure what perfect means, but she has some pictures in her head from her childhood fairy tales, movies, television, bridal magazines, her friends' weddings, and, of course, the ever-helpful wedding planner.

If the bride's parents are paying for it, maybe they're using a good portion of their retirement savings to give their adult daughter the wedding she's always wanted. A perfect wedding day is part of the bride's conditioning, not the groom's. Few grooms plan weddings. For him, it's performance art, a role he has to play to get through the event.

The average American wedding costs over $26,000. If the bride's family is picking up the tab, that lets the couple off the financial hook, except for the honeymoon. So strong is the pull of the perfect wedding that, if they are paying for it themselves, millions of couples begin married life with a shared debt, often carried on credit cards.

A great wedding is just that, an event which matched what the bride wanted on that day. It says nothing about the couple's ability to talk about money or plan together. It also shows little about whether a woman is ready to be a wife as much as she wants to be a bride. The little girl who wanted to marry the handsome prince and 'live happily ever after' did so after a perfect wedding.

I've often thought that it might be a good idea to let every woman have her wedding ceremony, then wait a year before she signs the papers that finalize the creation of a legal and financial unit. During this time, bride and groom can learn to discuss money and other realities of married life without the frenzy of wedding planning and the romantic illusions that cloud the ability to think beyond the event itself.

Myth 2:
Men are better with money than women.

How many times have we heard this one? And how many times have we repeated it? It's not true that men understand money matters better than women. They may tell us they do, and we have believed them. That becomes an expectation and we hand over responsibility. Even though the legal system that gave a husband power over his wife's money changed over a century ago, the mentality of too many women hasn't changed.

What is true is that until the last half century, men have had more experience with money. Their wages were higher; their education included mathematics; their professions dealt with numbers. The professions they chose paid more. They literally had more money to manage.

During that time, marriage was set up along the traditional model line with the husband in charge of the finances. More women stayed home, raised the children, ran the household and didn't pay much attention to the finances. Women didn't think they had a head for numbers, and let their husbands take responsibility for the community assets.

In the early '80s, Collette Dowling wrote *The Cinderella Complex*, a book exploring the deep-seated and often unrecognized desire of women to have men take care of them.

In the book, she describes her own experience of financial self-sabotage after she moved in with her boyfriend and expected him to take care of her needs. She writes about educated and resourceful women who marry and become helpless after 15 or 20 years of expecting their husband to handle all the finances. This is not true of all women all of the time, but enough to present a real problem if they are confronted with widowhood or divorce.

Cinderella, Snow White, Sleeping Beauty – all waiting for their prince to rescue them and make them happy. From Grimm to Disney, little girls wait for handsome princes to rescue them. One of the ways we do that is with an excuse cloaked as a biological imperative, i.e. men are better with numbers.

Unfortunately, rescue is not a financial strategy. The reality is that 85 of 100 women will spend part of their adult life on their own. Understanding numbers is part of being an adult.

Understanding money is not gender-specific. Not being involved can be dangerous and affect our well-being.

Myth 3:
Husbands have our best interests at heart.

Men don't marry to make women happy. They marry to make themselves happy. Keeping us happy is, if we're lucky, part of the equation.

Sometimes it isn't. It depends on whom you marry. A husband's best interests might involve power, control, ownership, status or just sheer bullying. Love is the stated reason, but men marry for a variety of reasons including regular sex, parenthood, becoming a member of the community, business reasons, and probably love. Few marry solely to make us happy, even though they may give lip service to doing so.

Quite honestly, we don't always know what our best interests are until we're in a situation where our internal caution lights flash. For example, my husband had a single-minded interest in the success of the company he was building.

I knew when we married that he was committed to that. In time, we expected to enjoy the fruits of his labor. We would travel, have fun and retire in good shape. In the meantime, he was willing to take financial risks that I didn't realize at the front end I would also be taking. I didn't understand that risks of such magnitude would be necessary in order for him to achieve his most important objective – the success of his business.

If I had understood what I was getting into, I might have made other choices about how to invest my own resources. For my husband, risk wasn't a sacrifice; it was what entrepreneurs did in the course of building their business. But because I had little control over company decisions, for me, the cyclical swings in finances often made me feel I was on a roller coaster.

When there were opportunities to secure outside capital, which would have lightened the financial load on us, my husband, like many company founders, was resistant to anyone other than himself controlling the destiny of the company. Selling the company wasn't even on his radar screen because he wanted his son to run it eventually. From where I stood, he didn't have my best interests at heart, nor was he working to make me happy.

Consider my daughter. She was married to a man who built a dream house for them in the middle of

20 beautiful acres in the foothills of the Sierra. Years later, when she decided to widen her horizons and go into a business of her own, the marriage foundered as her world widened. Her husband was incredulous that she didn't want to spend all her time in the forest with him, enjoying what he had built 'just' for her. They've been divorced for nearly a decade, and he still smarts at her lack of appreciation for the effort he put into building 'her house'.

Myth 4:
You Can Change Him After You Marry

No one can change another person unless that person wants to change. Does your husband have behaviors you don't like? If so, you can speak up and ask for change. You can't demand or expect that just because you want him to change, your husband will change for you. When you marry, you're taking on a fully-formed human influenced by experiences, people and events that very often you know little about.

If you marry without knowing him for a long enough period of time, you may be surprised to discover that what you see isn't what you thought you were getting. It's a strange thing about romance - we see what we want to see. The idealized image of our husband is superimposed on the person he really is.

That's one of the reasons that disappointment sets in after the first flush of romance is over. The problem is that some things you learn about later have a greater impact on your future well-being. For example, if you marry someone with a money style that varies greatly with your own, your whole financial life will be affected by what you didn't know about before you married.

We'll talk more about money styles later. But if you don't speak up about the things that bother you before marriage, they will continue to bother you after you're married.

Myth 5:
Husbands Need Romance

Men don't read Harlequin novels. There is no Modern Groom magazine. Men don't spend a year planning their wedding. Men 'do' romance because it makes us -- a girlfriend, fiancée or wife -- happier. It fulfills our need, not his. He uses romance to set the stage, to move him closer to what he really wants – sex, affection, closeness, and intimacy.

There's nothing wrong with that. It's just a strategy, and a smart one, at that. Strategy in support of a goal means that there is a plan to achieve it. When we say that a man is romantic, we're really saying that he knows the script and how to play his lines.

Some men are naturally more romantic. My husband wasn't one of them, but he had picked up enough cultural cues to understand that romance was important to me on certain occasions. Did he need the chocolates, flowers, trips, gifts that were part of my romantic scenario? Not likely. What he did need was to understand my ideas of how romance was supposed to work between us.

Myth 6:
Guilt is Inevitable

There are no perfect marriages. The good and bad co-exist, creating ambivalence for each of us. Anyone who says this isn't so is in denial. It's important to know this because if something does happen to your husband, you will feel guilty about this ambivalence.

When I interviewed widows as part of my research, I was struck by how their feelings of anger at their husband coexisted with their feelings of guilt. Closer questioning revealed that the guilt was related to things they wish they had understood, done or said to him before he died. They were left with unresolved issues and a lack of closure because they failed to raise subjects that were important to them.

When my husband died, I suffered the full range of pain associated with the death of someone I loved, but I experienced no guilt. Trauma, shock, disbelief, loss, grief, loneliness, invisibility, torpor, insomnia -- but no guilt. That's because we had explored the issues of unfinished business as part of the process of planning together. I didn't live with any 'if only, I should have, I could have, why didn't I' scenarios.

Chapter Seven

* * *

The Five Truths of Marriage

"Every form of refuge has its price."

The Eagles, "Lyin' Eyes"

Truth 1:
Marriages are recorded in court, not
in Heaven.

Marriages may be foretold in heaven, but when two people marry, that singular event registers at the courthouse here on earth. It creates one legal and financial unit called a couple. The couple part is misleading because there is actually a third partner in the marriage – the state, which from this point functions as a card carrying member of your marriage. The state bestows many contractual powers as well, which is one major reason that gays and lesbians want the right to marry.

The state cares about two things – that the event is recorded and that the tax collector knows where to send the bill. The public face of marriage may differ significantly from the private one, but the financial and legal obligations are the same until the court records that the marriage is no longer valid.

Even with one out of two marriages ending in divorce, marriage as an institution still receives greater respect from the community and carries a firmer commitment than living together. In a community property state, from the moment you say the words "I Do", all financial decisions that are made within the unit called your marriage belong to both of you, even if you don't know about them.

In many respects, marriage is like a business partnership. Not at all romantic, but true. What I want to highlight here is that most people going into a business partnership often understand their relationship better and know more about each other than two people who are getting married.

Business partners are, more often than not, on the 'same page'. They know what their product or service will be, understand the breakout of responsibilities, agree on a book keeping system which they both understand, review monthly financials together and keep tabs on the cash flow.

They don't make financial decisions without the other and they pick an accountant who has no ties with either partner. Personality and temperament can enter into the compatibility equation between them, and often, disrupt the ability of the partnership to function smoothly. But there's nothing in this relationship that has been shaped by the romance myth.

Imagine your business partner saying "Sign here, Honey" as he handed you a pen and a stack of papers. Surely you'd want to understand what you were signing. So you'd ask for more information about what the papers contained. If your partner dismissed your request by reassuring you that he'd taken care of everything, and you knew that you shared fifty percent of the liability for anything the partnership did, you'd want to know more.

Love and sex complicate partnerships. Partnerships operate in the real world and have clearer guidelines. Romance, love and sex are governed by myths, expectations, disappointments, and a river of emotions that bathe decisions in unconscious sabotage.

Truth 2:
Husbands Can't Read Minds.

Actually, no one can. It's not anyone's job to intuit that you want or need something. This is one of the myths that swirl around romance – "if he really loves me, he knows what I want." How can he know that?

He didn't learn it from his mother who probably behaved the same way you are and didn't ask for what she wanted or needed either. His father may have been clueless about what his mother wanted for the same reason.

So how is a man going to 'know' what you or I or anyone else needs unless we tell him? And how will he know that we want or need it again, and again, unless we tell him that, too? It's irritating, I know. Women instinctively understand what other women need and want because they can more easily put themselves in our shoes.

I've never heard a man complain about his wife by saying, "If she really loved me, she'd know what I want." Speaking up about what we need or want isn't the problem. It's how we do that and what we say and how we say it.

Truth 3:
It's Not Romantic to Talk about Money.

Nor is it romantic to talk about the plumbing, fixing the car, how long your mother will visit next month or any of the myriad of other topics that are part of married life. Why does money get the bad rap here? More importantly, why should something as basic as money be abandoned to the world of the romantic?

You might think that I have a problem with romance. On the contrary, I love the fun, excitement, spirit of adventure and the energy and fascination of romance. I just don't think it's a good framework for discussions about nuts and bolts subjects like money, financial planning, responsibility, or the plumbing.

There are many dictionary definitions for the word romance, among them "fictitious," "fanciful" and "without basis in fact." Financial problems rank as the top reason for divorce. It makes sense for money to be a priority for discussion before and during marriage.

Truth 4:
Death is not a Four-Letter Word.

No matter who you are, no matter what you've achieved, whether you are happy and healthy, God-fearing or atheist, rich or poor, you will die. So will your spouse. If you were to be widowed, the laws of the state reflect nothing about the quality of the relationship you had with your husband. At that point, it's all about the law.

Death can happen in 'a moment, or be prolonged over time if your husband is ill. Because death has real and practical consequences for survivors, denying that it will happen cheats survivors of the ability to plan.

Obviously, the best time to discuss this last taboo is *before you need it.* Failing to do so will put you at the mercy of the state, your children or stepchildren, your husband's attorney and accountant, and possibly, an ex-wife or two. Because statistics show that you will probably outlive your husband, it would be smart for you to know what you need to know before you are widowed. This willingness to plan with you could be one of the greatest acts of love your husband will ever demonstrate. If he has difficulty facing his mortality, recognize that in this situation, you have to be the stronger one.

Truth 5:
There are no guarantees in marriage or in life.

When something good or bad happens to us, it could just as easily have been otherwise. Statisticians spend careers amassing vast quantities of information about everything in our culture. Where we are at any given moment on a statistician's chart or graph can change with or without our consent. The statistics don't reflect anything personal. All they do is quantify what's happening to segments of the population.

The odds of something bad happening to us is always fifty percent. Unless we lead a very sheltered life, rarely venturing from home (and even then, we are never completely 'safe'), we can't intentionally avoid, defer, bargain, placate, postpone or trade-off destiny, though you'd never know it by how hard we try.

Ultimately, all we can do is recognize that there are no guarantees and plan accordingly. For instance, how about facing our own mortality by having a will, a living trust, appointing a guardian for the children, letting the children know we've done that, telling people we love that we love them? And that's just for starters.

Fate being what it is, it might make good sense to learn about net-worth, budgets, investments, long term care insurance (so the kids don't go bankrupt keeping us alive at the end of our life), which documents we need to keep on hand in case our husband dies, etc.

Some mutual planning is definitely in order. For example, what's the best way to introduce difficult subjects like death and disability? What should you know about setting up a trust, what end of life issues do you need to discuss (some funerals cost as much as weddings!), what should your obituary say if you die first, what do you need to know about your husband's money, and other taboo subjects that we avoid talking about.

The more you procrastinate in discussing these and related subjects, the greater the odds that something will happen that you're not ready for...and the higher the anxiety about discussing these things will become. If you've read this far, I don't have to tell you that anxiety may well keep you from ever having the conversation.

Chapter Eight

***

Even Handsome Princes Die

"Between grief and nothing, I choose grief."

William Faulkner

When I was interviewing widows as part of my research, I noted that many were still angry at their husband – for dying, for leaving them with a financial mess, for not fulfilling the dreams they had shared when they married.

Many also felt guilty, even after many years of being on their own, for not expressing their feelings when they could have. A few told me that if they could do it all over again, they would tell their husband what was really on their mind.

At first, I considered their comments interesting, but not directly related to the research I was doing. Yet the more I thought about it, the more I realized how much their angry feelings about the lack of financial intimacy in their marriage kept them from experiencing intimacy in other areas of their marriage. Their silence simmered under the surface and created resentment and a lack of trust. When their husbands died, their healing process was clouded by their continuing preoccupation with their unresolved feelings and regrets.

On the morning of September 11, 2001, I watched in horror with the rest of the world as planes crashed into the World Trade Center. As the morning progressed and the twin towers collapsed in a fiery heap of smoke and ashes, one of my over-riding thoughts was "Did the survivors have a chance to say 'I love you' that morning when their loved ones left for work? Did survivors leave the house angry that morning? Did the people who died know how much they were loved and appre-ciated? Did the survivors know how much they meant to the people who died? Or would the survivors carry, in addition to the pain and grief of loss, the awareness that they never said the things they might have wanted to say if they had known life could be so short?"

All my life, I've been aware of the risk that people will die without having the chance to speak to each other from the heart. Some in my own family were given a second chance after years of bad blood between them. My father and his sister were estranged for 25 years because of a silly disagreement that put their egos on the line. When his sister was dying of cancer, my father visited her in the hospital every day. The first visit was painful for them both, but with each successive visit, they relaxed into a familiarity they hadn't known since childhood. They had the chance to understand, to forgive, to let go of the hurts and to appreciate the years of love they had shared.

I loved my husband, but our marriage wasn't perfect. I don't know what a perfect marriage looks or feels like. No one I know appears to have one. Maybe there is no such thing. On balance, my husband and I had more happy times than unhappy ones. We'd disagree, argue, fight, make-up – not an unusual cycle of married life.

Because I was aware of the suddenness with which life could change, I decided to write a series of questions into the seminar I was preparing for women. The questions deal with things a husband and wife might want to say to each other if they thought they might never see each other again.

I needed to test them out and asked my husband to participate in that process with me. We had never given each other permission to be so honest with each other. My husband hated open-ended conversations about 'our relationship'. He felt we went around in circles instead of doing what he was most comfortable with, i.e. stating what the problem was and what I wanted him to do about it or vice versa.

This process I was asking him to participate in was different. It hit the emotional areas that needed airing, but it was in a different context. It didn't require any conversational feedback; therefore, it wouldn't go 'round in circles. It seems eerily prescient that we had the chance to complete the process not long before he died.

When my husband died, I suffered the anguish and loss that accompanies the death of someone I loved, but no guilt. I didn't live with any 'if only, I should have, I could have, why I didn't' scenarios. We had written each other letters in which we had answered the questions that follow.

On a separate sheet of paper, write out your answers to the questions that follow. Be honest. These answers are just for you right now. Then tuck the paper away until later in this book. You'll be surprised and comforted by what you come up with. Please trust me. I know this process works.

The Process

Imagine that your husband has died. Imagine that you are looking at his coffin or the urn with his ashes. Imagine that you could write him a letter that he could somehow still understand – a letter about yourself, him, your marriage, and the life you shared. Remember, you'll never see him again except in your heart and mind.

Honest answers to these questions will give you a clearer look at your own feelings. Feelings aren't rational or irrational, good or bad. They're just feelings. Don't censor yourself...let your feelings run. No one will see this letter. If you don't feel like answering all the questions, answer just a few. You may want to get back to them later. You don't have to speak them, or share them, or show them to anyone.

- What were the good parts about your marriage and what were the bad?

- Did your husband know that you loved and respected him?

- Did he know why?

- Did he know that you might be angry with him?

- Did he know why?

- What did you ask him for that he wouldn't give you?

- What did you need that he didn't listen to?

- What did you withhold from him that you knew he wanted from you?

- What do you wish you had said while you still could?

- What made you fall in love with him?

- What did you admire, respect and like about him?

- Is there anything you would have changed if you realized you could?

- What do you regret doing or not doing?

- Is there anything you want to thank him for?

After you write out your answers, tuck them away. We'll come back to them later in the book.

Chapter Nine

✳ ✳ ✳

Romance vs. Reality

> "...When the lovely flame dies,
> smoke gets in your eyes."
>
> *Jerome Kern*

In the early 1960s, there was a television program called "Queen for a Day." Jack Bailey, the master of ceremonies, would start the show by shouting: "Would YOU like to be Queen for a Day?" "YES," the audience screamed back.

The game went like this: Bailey interviewed four women on each show. Whichever woman's life was deemed in the worst shape by the audience applause meter was crowned Queen for A Day. The audience cried their eyes out, morbidly delighted to find there were people worse off than they were.

Even though it was the worst sort of entertainment, I and millions of other mothers settled in for a half hour of escape. The host draped the Queen in a sable-trimmed red velvet robe and placed a jeweled crown on her head. She cried with joy as she was showered with gifts from manufacturers eager to get their products in front of their target market.

What had she done to deserve all this? Nothing. She was just the most miserable of all the contestants that day.

I never coveted the washer or dryer, refrigerator, Mixmaster, or new car. Instead, I was mesmerized by the vicarious experience of romance, of being chosen and honored and gifted. I wanted life to be not as it was, but as I wanted it to be.

So millions of us, mothers with babies isolated in our little houses in the suburbs, cried with the Queen, for her, for ourselves, not knowing that we were dealing with what Betty Freidan would later call 'the problem with no name.'

For me, that half hour of vicarious escape was more exciting even than my wedding, which by then had become a distant historical event, archived in a maroon leather-bound photo album stored out of reach on the bookcase's highest shelf. What I remember vividly, even today, was how romantic it felt to identify with this woman, miserable though she was. Nothing like my real world as a wife and mother, with its labyrinth of obligations, restrictions, expectations. In my wildest dreams, I couldn't have envisioned the contrast between my wedding day and my life as a wife and mother.

I've long held the suspicion that women would rather be a bride than a wife. I know I did. I had no idea what it meant to be a wife other than that's what I would be called after my wedding. Being a bride has all the romance of being queen for a day. You are showered with gifts. You are the center of attention as family, friends, bridegroom and an army of bridal industry specialists spend countless hours to ensure that you're given a perfect day. The collective obsession with romance affirms that if you spend enough money to make everything 'perfect,' your marriage will be perfect.

What's the harm of suspending reality for just one magical day? Of course the bride knows that the wedding has to be paid for by someone, preferably her father, but too often, the new couple is willing to begin married life with a financial liability of $26,327, which is the average cost of a wedding in 2005, according to the Fairchild Bridal Group. The belief attached to this outrageous expenditure, no matter who pays for it, is simple – the little girl inside wants fulfillment for something she has been waiting for since she played with her Barbie doll.

The problem isn't that women don't understand that our deepest, most childish fairy tale dreams are being exploited in the $125 billion dollar wedding industry. The real problem is that we like the fairy tale, especially the one where the glass slipper fits only on one foot – ours. The truth is, you can't walk very far in a glass slipper.

For women, a little romance goes a long way. It takes so little to stimulate that part of our brain which we connect with romance. Give us a few cues, and we rush in to fill in the blanks because, culturally, we recognize the script. We know how the story is supposed to end. We are going to live happily ever after. That's what the fairy tales say. That's what the romance novels say.

Here's an example of how tightly we cling to the idea of happily ever after.

After the morning break in one of my seminars, I noticed that Stephanie, a pretty brunette in her late twenties, had not returned. She had come with her mother, Rosalie, who had paid for Stephanie's registration. Rosalie wanted her daughter, who was to be married in a few months, to learn before marriage what Rosalie had learned the hard way after a bitter and rancorous divorce.

Not wanting to keep the other women waiting, I asked Rosalie where Stephanie was. She said, "Stephanie left. She said she didn't want her romantic illusions shattered."

This was an amazing thing to me. Here was a woman who would soon be a wife, who knew she had illusions which I assume had to do with her future husband or marriage – and yet she wanted to hold on to them. This wasn't denial where she didn't know that she didn't know. It wasn't the ostrich syndrome where she thought she was safe because she closed her eyes. Stephanie's eyes were open. She knew she had romantic illusions, and she wanted to keep them. Why?

Years after my wedding, I would watch my daughters play with their Barbie and Ken dolls, re-enacting the couple's wedding day. Even at seven years old, my girls knew what the perfect wedding should look like.

What does romance mean? We know it when we see it; we feel it, we crave it, we need it. But what does the word actually mean? Take a look at some of the dictionary definitions:

- Involving or characteristic of a love affair or sexual love, especially when the relationship is idealized or exciting or intense

- Relating to or characterized by a fascination or enthusiasm for something, especially of an uncritical or indefinable kind
- Relating to or characterized by adventure, excitement, the potential for heroic achievement and the exotic
- Characterized by or arising from idealistic or impractical attitudes and expectations

––––––––––––––––

In a wonderful cartoon by Hilary Price, a man is kneeling in front of the woman, holding an open jewelry box with an engagement ring. The caption reads, "Let's assume each other's debt, trade in our independence for security and societal approval, and celebrate with an event that will have cost overruns in the thousands."

At this writing, there are five monthly bridal magazines. Two of them, Modern Bride and Bride's Magazine, weigh in at three pounds and contain nearly 800 pages of products and services devoted to ensuring the bride has a perfect wedding. Pages burst with photos and pitches from advertisers selling bridal gowns, venues for wedding ceremonies and honeymoon hideaways, caterers, beauty salons, household appliances, lines, florists, stationery and the hundreds of details that appear on the bride's to do list. Editorial content deals with wedding gift etiquette, beauty tips, catering ideas, table decorations, choosing a tuxedo and other topics related to the "Big Day."

Noticeably absent is any information about the financial nature of marriage – budgeting, dealing with money conflicts, checking accounts, separate and community property, prenuptial and postnuptial agreements and the myriad of other financial details that couples will grapple with once they are married. There are no ads for insurance and financial services companies, legal or accounting firms.

Why should there be? This is not their target market. It's as if the wedding day is the successful end point of a journey rather than the portal to a new and entirely separate phase of life.

Men don't crave romance. Romance is what women crave – and smart husbands take it seriously. We can't always define it, but we know it when we see it. On some level, romance lies dormant in a woman's heart, waiting to be kindled, and for most of us, rekindled. It doesn't seem to matter that romance is illusion. We believe it anyway.

How unromantic, you might say, to treat marriage with the clear-eyed, logical and practical approach we would take if we were considering a business venture. In truth, most brides don't. Who wants to take the chance of bringing up a subject that, in the past, might have made our groom impatient, even angry?

"Why are you always thinking about money?" he asked when you tried one more time to discuss how you will be handling finances. "Didn't we agree to talk about that after the honeymoon?" Who wants to spoil the euphoria of wedding plans and the fantasy and excitement of the honeymoon by discussing money? So mundane. So unromantic. But so intimate, nevertheless. What is more real or more intimate than disclosing and understanding our fifty percent responsibility for the well-being of our real world union?

Whether we like it or not, marriage has many of the same components as a business partnership. One partner doesn't make the financial decisions for both. The financial records are open for both to see and understand. Financial commitments are understood and agreed to by both. Each is responsible for their share of the business.

Marriage	Business/ Partnership
Income	Income
Expenses	Expenses
Assets	Assets
Liabilities	Liabilities
Taxes	Taxes
Net Worth	Net Worth
Expectations	Job descriptions
Relatives	Managers
Friends	Consultants
Romance	Real Time

Notice how a marriage and business partnership resemble each other in above-the-line items:

- Income is the total amount of money that comes in during the year.

- Expenses is the sum total of monies spent during that same year.

- Assets represent what the marriage or the partnership owns.

- Liabilities are debts of either the marriage or the partnership. Whatever isn't already paid for is a liability.

- Taxes are what Uncle Sam charges either the marriage or the partnership based on what the income and expenses have been during the year. These taxes come in the form of income and property taxes.

- Net worth is calculated by subtracting what you both owe – the liabilities – from what you both own – the assets. The difference between the numbers is your Net Worth. If you live in one of the community property states, half of the net worth– 50 percent- belongs to you. Your spouse or partner owns the other fifty percent.

What throws this relationship off balance is what happens below the line. Here lie the emotional pitfalls, the subliminal scripts, the dramas and the disappointments.

Let's look at the expectations versus the job description. It's easy to work with a job description.

It has a set of tasks that can be defined; they're visible and usually measurable with regard to some kind of result. If we're not doing what the job description says we should be doing, our boss will let us know that we're off-track. We have some choices here: get back on track, quit our job or get fired. It's job description vs. job performance, with no love lost as part of this equation.

What about relatives/friends versus managers/consultants? In a business, if you run into a problem you can't solve on your own, you hire outside people to help you. Chances are you would have a clear idea of what the problem is and you would want to have the problem solved because you are paying money to these outside sources.

Theoretically, these outside sources have no vested interest in supporting either your point of view or that of your partner. If you're doing something counterproductive, chances are you'd do it differently to help solve the problem. That's not how we do things in marriage. Either we don't ask for feedback from 'outside' consultants, or if we do, and they provide it, we expect it to support our view of things. Even worse, we usually consult friends or relatives who 'are on our side' and who may have their own agenda.

What about romance versus real time operation for a business? Imagine a business plan that includes any of the components of romance. Except perhaps for the adventure and excitement of watching a business grow, any idealistic, impractical attitudes or fictitious or fanciful expectations will put the business out of business in very short order.

How unromantic to even think this way. But this

is the price of realizing that marriage is a legal and financial undertaking as well as a love match. And Uncle Sam doesn't give a hoot if it works or not. Whether a marriage ends, either through widowhood or divorce, or a business fails, legal and financial details need to be resolved. At this point, it's too late to do things differently.

When you achieve financial intimacy, you create financial transparency, just as you would expect in a partnership. If your marriage ends because of death or divorce, and you don't know what was going on while you were one-half of this partnership, you could be left with a legal and financial mess. At the very least, you may not have the protection you need to rebuild your life.

I'm not advocating that romance be abolished. Romance is fun, but it's based on fiction. Intimacy on the other hand, is a deeper thrill, a more mature bond that says, "I trust you, I want you to know what's real, I want you to participate with me in shaping our life together." It's the ultimate connection with another person.

I want you to consider separating the fanciful from the practical, the emotions from the money, and the romance from the intimacy. Like oil and water, they don't mix. What you can do, and should do for your own protection, is recognize that going into a partnership expected to last for the rest of your life requires full participation in order to work in the long run. Not knowing about your joint finances means you're not playing an equal role in making decisions. It can leave you feeling dependent and vulnerable, and in reality, you will be.

Chapter Ten

* * *

Five Financial Mistakes Wives Make

"What's love got to do with it?"

Tina Turner

A wise friend suggested that you can learn a lot about a man by asking him to describe his mother, the first role model a man has for how women behave.

My husband's mother was one of the first Certified Public Accountants in California. She was a single mom and supported him and his siblings on her income. When we met, my independence and desire to build my own business fit right into the image he had of what women are supposed to be. For me, it was a refreshing change from my first marriage, where my husband wanted a wife who would be at his side as he climbed the corporate ladder.

Deciding how you and your husband will divide your money is between the two of you. But be forewarned: money issues don't go away. They just get more so. Here are some of the more common mistakes. I hate to admit it, but I made most of them.

Mistake 1:
"Sign Here Honey"

Probably every wife has heard these three little words at some time. Most of the time we don't think about it. We figure if it's good for him, it's good for us, especially if we live in a community property state. He wouldn't do anything to jeopardize our finances. What we don't realize when we sign is that we are taking on one-half of the debt incurred if something goes wrong with what we're signing.

So far, nothing wrong with that. It's a marriage. Co-signing is fair. It's above board. It's what happens in partnerships. The problem arises when there is no discussion about what is being signed.

In a business partnership, there is likely to be discussion of any output of money or taking on of debt. Certainly there is an income tax filing for the partnership to which both parties attest to the accuracy of the information. A business partner would not dream of sliding papers under the other's nose and saying "Sign here." The other partner would surely want to know what it was, what it was for, and how much it would cost before signing. Marriage, as much a business partnership as anything else, too often doesn't work that way.

Consider Jane's story:

"My husband asked me to sign some papers for a house refinancing. We had done that before for a

lower mortgage rate and it didn't seem like a big deal. He wanted to get some money out of the house to diversify investments. That seemed like a good idea; he'd been doing our investments over the years. What I didn't know was that he had what he considered a hot stock tip, a chance to buy Priceline.com while the stock was rising. When the dot-com bubble burst, the stock plummeted. He still believed in it and didn't sell it soon enough. I didn't find out about it until tax time when we went to the accountant and I learned that what I thought would be our retirement savings of $500,000 was lost. My husband was very apologetic, he didn't mean to hurt us, and he was doing something he thought was right. I was furious. It wasn't the loss so much as that he didn't ask or involve me. I felt victimized. He had taken a chance with my future, too – and we both lost."

The tax return you and your husband file every year is the ultimate 'Sign here, Honey' transaction. Even women who earn in the six figures, often managing the finances and budgets of corporations and hundreds of employees, sometimes find themselves acting in the traditional role of wife – and letting their husband handle the finances at home.

My friend Marge is a decorating consultant and runs her own business. Because she is sole proprietor, she isn't accustomed to consulting anyone about her own business decisions. When her husband Steve filed for divorce, Marge realized for the first time that she had signed their joint tax returns without ever glancing at them. When I interviewed her, she shared an excerpt from her divorce deposition with me:

Q: Did you see the tax returns every year?

A: Yes.

Q: Did you review them before you signed them?

A: No, I didn't. I trusted Steve completely.

Q: Weren't you curious, whether you trusted him or not, about the state of your finances?

A: Frankly, no.

Q: Did you ever keep copies of the returns which you signed?

A: I didn't. Steve kept all the papers."

In addition to tax returns that Steve filed without the help of an accountant, Marge discovered loan papers she knew nothing about and promissory notes for which she was responsible, even after they were divorced. Steve hadn't told Marge about some of the business deals he'd been involved with. Moreover, Marge had a bookkeeper who handled the details of Marge's business. At tax time, she pulled the information together for Marge who gave it to Steve for inclusion on their joint tax return. Had they been working with an accountant, Marge would have learned more about Steve's financial activities and that he was involved in some deals he hadn't told her about before.

When anyone asks you to sign something, you need to understand what you're signing, and if you don't, you ask for more information. But too often when a husband says, "Sign here honey" and you want to know more, he can stop you with a put-down like "Don't you trust me?" or the combative "Why do you suddenly want to know?" Or, he might say "Don't worry about a thing dear," thus tapping into your mindset to let him take care of you. This is benefliction in action and not guaranteed always to be in your best interests.

Most things don't require an immediate signature, so don't sign anything you don't understand. You are entitled to ask for a copy of whatever you will be expected to sign. That means loan papers, contracts for services or purchases, and especially, the tax returns. It's better if you and your husband are working with an accountant. You should definitely be part of that process. If you've decided that you're fine with him keeping the records, it's imperative that you have access to them. You don't want to learn about any of these financial matters after a death or divorce.

Mistake 2:
Putting separate funds into joint ventures

Another mistake wives make is putting inherited money, which is considered your separate property even if you are married when you inherit it, into a joint account. On the face of it, there's nothing wrong with that. The problems occur, however, if something happens to the marriage because of death or divorce.

Once separate funds are put into a community property investment or other community asset, the funds co-mingle. Unless you are keeping a clear paper trail, with itemized receipts for your share of what you put in, it is hard to tease apart the value of your separate property investment.

For example, after I was divorced from my first husband, I received half of our community property. I had the funds to put the down payment on the home my second husband and I had built at Lake Tahoe. My husband wrote out the checks for the mortgage every month. We co-owned the property, and he made the payments from our joint account. However, when his company needed a loan, and the property was pledged as collateral, I didn't ask the company to reimburse me for the value of the down payment. The house was pledged as community property against the business over which I had little control.

Did I trust my husband? Yes. Did I know he wanted what was best for us? Yes. But the well-being of his company was his top priority. I knew that if the company did well, we would both benefit.

But, there was a natural assumption on his part that if it was his priority, it was also mine. I simply didn't understand the danger of not having the company, a corporation and separate entity, provide me with compensation for using the house as collateral. I wasn't involved in the company's decisions. The company's treasurer didn't think about my needs, and I didn't know enough about what I should ask for to get the property secured. A few years later, after the property was sold, the money again went to pay off a business obligation. My down payment was gone.

Mistake 3:
Avoiding 'Money Talk'

If money is a loaded topic, as it is for so many couples, then there's never going to be a good time to talk about it. But talk about it we must.

To some degree, most of us harbor irrational attitudes toward money. If we thought logically about money, we'd be able to live fairly consistent and well-balanced financial lives. Our logic would go along the lines of earn more, spend less, budget, save for retirement, pay estimated taxes on time, buy low, sell high. Ask for the raise. Use the money to protect ourselves and bring us pleasure. Share it with those we love and with those who need it. Money would be like electricity or water – a form of energy that makes other things happen.

It's the "other things happen" part of this equation where we get into trouble. We have all kinds of emotions wrapped around money that aren't at all about money. Those emotions create attitudes about money which are influenced by many factors and variables over the course of many years. They in turn shape us. By the time we marry, we have expectations about money that run head-on into the attitudes and money style of our husband.

Mistake 4:
Letting your husband keep the records

Let's say you are involved in all the financial decisions, but you and your husband have decided that he will handle the monthly details: the real estate paperwork, the monthly statements from the bank, investment and credit card companies, loan repayment statements, receipts for items bought with cash, the tax returns, updated financial profiles. So far, fine.

Your husband may have a filing system that works for him, and you don't understand it. Or he may use a computer program to keep track of everything, but you don't understand how it works. Or he may have a login password that you don't know. Even worse, he may keep the records in his office, thereby severely limiting your access to the financial information you would need immediately in case he were to be ill, or died suddenly.

You need a copy of everything that involves your joint financial activities. If your husband doesn't like you going into his filing system, get copies of the paperwork you need to keep and start your own filing system. If your husband is being above board about the finances, there's no reason he wouldn't want you to understand everything you're both involved in.

If your husband is involved with financial decisions that affect his separate property (which presumably you know about because you discussed it before marriage), he has the right to make decisions without consulting you. If you own separate property and you've decided to keep it separate, you have that same right.

For example, let's say you're in a second marriage and your husband has a condo which remains his separate property. Let's say he decides to renovate the condo and has sufficient funds in his account to handle the renovation. As long as he doesn't use any of the community funds to invest, he can do anything he wants. You don't have to track those records unless and until he taps into some of the community property funds to handle the renovation. You have a right to know how much of your community funds are being used to invest in his separate property.

There are certain payments that you should

never leave up to your husband without at least asking about them. For example, Anna's husband paid their bills at the last minute. He liked the feeling of riding the float and keeping the money in their account as long as possible. It made Anna uncomfortable, but she decided not to make an issue out of it.

One morning, her husband was killed on his way to work when an uninsured driver ran a red light at an intersection and broadsided his car. She contacted the company from whom they had bought a term life insurance policy. The payment was late; the company had cancelled the policy. It was all in the small print of the insurance contract. Anna had no legal ground to stand on.

One of the elements of our estate plan was for my husband to be insured under a 'key man policy' for the company. The premium would be paid by the accounts payable department. Unfortunately, the company treasurer, whom I never really trusted to watch out for my interests, determined the timetable for bills to be paid. My husband thought I was being a little unreasonable when every month, I asked for confirmation that the premium had been paid.

The treasurer wouldn't have lost any sleep if the premium payment had been delayed. He could have covered another bill that in his judgment needed to be paid sooner, such as paying a supplier in a shorter time to get a discount. I had no leverage to influence the treasurer's decision. I nagged my husband to get the reassurance we both needed that our personal safety wasn't being jeopardized by the business decisions of someone else who had no personal risk in the business.

Participating in the financial decisions and keeping copies of your records is only one part of the equation. You need to keep copies of any changes that affect your financial situation. You'll find information about what you need to keep later in this book.

Mistake 5:
Paying an equal share when your financial situation changes.

When I married the first time, my husband and I started from square one financially. Whatever assets we accumulated, we did it together. Not so with my second marriage. I had assets; my husband had separate assets. We agreed to share expenses by contributing equally to the community pot and keep what was left over for our separate accounts.

My husband, as head of his company, could adjust his salary, and often did. When the interest rate on our adjustable rate mortgage for the house was low, I had no trouble covering my share. However, a rise in the interest rate and a higher monthly mortgage payment came at a time when my business took a nose dive during the recession of the mid '80s. My husband had to pick up the slack. He felt I wasn't doing my share financially. It didn't occur to me then that I had already done more than my share by providing that very first down payment years before. I had never been reimbursed for that money by his company, even though the residence was listed on my husband's financial statement and used as collateral for extensions of business credit.

I didn't understand at the time how important it

was to be really clear, open and honest about money and our feelings about how we spend it. We finally settled on a ratio of what each of us could afford to pay based on income that was actually coming in. Because the finances were transparent, meaning that neither of us was holding anything back from each other, we were able to come up with something that worked for both of us.

Chapter Eleven

* * *

Mistakes Widows and Divorcees Make

"Trust, but verify."

Ronald Reagan

I f you are widowed or divorced, and you marry again, the chances are that you will think about and handle money issues the same way you did in your previous marriage. This time however, you may have more assets than you did when you married before. Here are some things to be aware of if you date or intend to marry again.

Mistake 1:
Handing financial responsibility to someone else.

One of the most important messages of this book is that you learn what you need to know about your finances before you are in a situation where you have to manage on your own. If your husband handled the finances in your marriage, and you are now divorced or widowed, it will feel tempting to let the new man in your life take charge of your money. You may think he makes better decisions than you can about what you need.

Take things slowly. Don't make any investment decisions until you understand what you are doing and why you are doing it. You need to be able to explain things to yourself and not just take your new boyfriend or husband's or a financial advisor's word for financial decisions. If you can't do that, you will be dependent on someone other than yourself. You will be vulnerable to the decisions others are making for you.

Educate yourself about the reason someone is steering you in a certain direction. Try to determine if the person advising you has a vested interest in your following the recommendations he or she provides. Get used to participating with, and not handing over responsibility for, your well-being to someone else, whether they are your children, a financial advisor, a new man, a friend, anyone. No one has your best interests at heart the way you do.

Once the pain of loss subsides, and you can think clearly again, then talk with a financial advisor or planner. Read books about managing your money. *Remember this - anyone who makes money off of your money is not a disinterested party.* This person's income often depends on your following the advice they give you because they make money from sales of a product or service to you.

Find a financial advisor who will charge you by the hour without tying up your funds in investments you don't understand. You will know when you are thinking clearly and ready to take a more active role in working with the advisor on your finances (more about this later)

Mistake 2:
Boosting his ego.

Let's say you're dating Bob, a man you really like. You think your relationship may have a future. You've been on some lovely trips together and he's been generous and gracious in picking up the tab. You have no reason to doubt that he is financially successful: he drives a Lexus, wears Armani suits, is knowledgeable about wine and food at the best restaurants and loves the same things you do. It appears that he is what wealth advisors and counselors call a 'fiscally equal' situation.

Bob is very enthusiastic about helping you with your money. He has some ideas which he is certain will result in great gain for you. It's very tempting – you see each other frequently and besides, Bob's ideas seem to make sense. He is very patient in how he explains things to you, making you feel less intimidated by the subject of money management.

Bob feels rebuffed that you're not more open to disclosing your financial situation to him. You're feeling that pressure; you don't want to hurt his feelings and you certainly don't want to jeopardize a lovely relationship.

Touchy situation, right?

Actually, no. The only time Bob should even know about your assets is if your relationship is moving towards commitment. At that point, you'd both be disclosing financial information about yourselves to each other. You would see if Bob's affluence was real because you'd be sharing financial profiles. Sharing profiles doesn't mean combining assets. But you'll learn a lot about whether Bob is someone whose advice you could follow.

Mistake 3:
Over-spending.

Maybe you'll remarry, maybe not. What you need to do is work with someone who can help you set guidelines for budgeting and investing. I'm not a financial counselor or planner, but I urge you to work with one, especially if your husband handled everything while you were married.

Keep in mind that settling an estate or receiving a divorce settlement may be the first time that you have a sum of money to work with that is yours and yours alone. It's tempting to spend on things you've always wanted, especially if your husband called the financial shots. Suddenly, there is no one who can deny you what you want. If you're working with a large amount of money, then buying and living the way you want may not be a problem at first.

But in order to make the money meet your needs over the years, it's important to invest it. The more you spend of the principal, the less you have to invest and earn for you. You'll be working out the right proportion of spending to investing with your financial advisor. I'm just calling your attention now to the temptation presented by a sizeable amount of money you may inherit because of life insurance or proceeds from the settlement of your estate.

The same caveat applies to lending money to your adult children without some agreement about them paying you back or you having some interest in how they are using your money. You must ask yourself: if your children are a good credit risk, why are they coming to you, especially since you are going to need to invest the money to take care of yourself so that you don't become a burden to them as you age? Couldn't they just go to a bank and get a loan?

Let's be realistic about this. Your children might not qualify as a good credit risk with the bank. You will feel emotionally vulnerable after you are widowed. You may be lonely and your children offer you the comfort of love and companionship. You may feel guilty that you have money while they have all these financial burdens which you could help alleviate if you gave them money. Your maternal instincts might kick in to help them pay off maxed-out credit cards, etc. You may feel selfish not sharing with them. Recognize that you may feel all of that. It's normal and natural to feel that way, and it won't kill you.

If your children need money for a down payment on a house, a business venture, a boat, or whatever, make sure your name is on the title with them. Ask your attorney about the best way to do that. If you lend them money without an agreement for repayment, that's as good as giving them a gift, which is fine, as long as you don't expect to recoup your money. If your name is also on the property, at least you have an interest in it if it needs to be sold. Verbal agreements, handshakes, promises – all terrific, and all not legal and not binding.

You also need to set up a payment schedule for getting the money repaid. It's important for your children to repay the loan because it makes them more financially responsible. Waive the interest if you're feeling generous, but insist that the principal be paid back on time, just as they would have to pay back the bank. You see, you are acting in place of a bank. Except you're a lot easier because you're not running a credit check on them. You know their history working with money. You want to maintain close loving relationships with them. You want to continue to see your grandkids. You place all that in jeopardy when you lend children money.

Most importantly, if you need the money, don't make the loan! Who wants to initiate legal action against our children? But I've seen just that happen. Even after completing a legal agreement with your children, there's still the danger of not being repaid. You be the judge on this one, but be sure to go in with your eyes open.

Part Three

Getting Intimate About Money

Community Property States

Arizona

California

Idaho

Louisiana

Nevada

New Mexico

Texas

Washington

Wisconsin

Chapter Twelve

✳ ✳ ✳

Money Talk Before Marriage

"For money has the power above
The stars and fate to manage love."

Samuel Butler

Before you read the next chapter, take this short personal quiz regarding your finances. It will give you a clearer picture about what you already know about your own finances or, if you're already married, your joint finances.

Your home

The current value of my home is _____.

My mortgage is _____.

The equity in my home is _____.

The mortgage payment schedule is _____.

The interest payment on my mortgage is _____.

My insurance coverage is _____.

The deductible on my homeowner's insurance is _____.

Personal Finance

My salary minus monthly deductions is _____.

My husband's salary minus monthly deductions is _____.

We save _____ percent of our monthly income.

My credit card debt is _____.

My husband's credit card debt is _____.

Insurance

The coverage of my (my husband's) life insurance is _____.

The cost (monthly, annual) of the insurance is _____.

Health insurance cost and coverage _____.

Disability insurance cost _____.

I carry an umbrella insurance policy for $_____ that costs $_____ annually.

Taxes

I reviewed my tax return with the person who prepared it. Yes _____ No _____

Investments

Location and amounts of Cash, CDs, Stocks and Bonds, Real Estate:

_____

_____

_____

Amount of return on above investments:

_____

_____

_____

What we're investing in together:

_____

_____

What we're investing in with separate funds:

_____

_____

The Family Business

Current Valuation of Business $_____.

Debt $_____.

Liquid Assets $_____.

Succession Planning
Yes _____   No _____

Retirement

Social Security
With my spouse / Without my spouse

_____

Pension Fund – Who is it with, how much is in it, who is beneficiary?

_____

Retirement accounts – IRA, Keogh, 401K - amount, location:

_____

_____

Years ago, I attended a workshop called Money and You. For one of the exercises, participants were given a newly printed $100 bill and two silver dollars. We were told to tear the bill in half and chew it. The silver dollars we were to toss into a dumpster behind the building. Most of us couldn't do either of those things. For me, the thought of chewing on green paper was nauseating. Tearing a $100 bill in half was something I also couldn't bring myself to do, although some of the participants had less trouble with that one. Toss two silver dollars in a dumpster? They're crazy.

The purpose of the exercise was to demonstrate that money – the thing itself – is neutral, an inanimate object, a piece of paper or chunk of metal. That holds true for a diamond or a piece of gold. We're not likely to want to suck on any of them. Neither gold, diamonds or money have real value in keeping us warm, nourished or sheltered. What they do have is symbolic value because we as a society agree that they do. The real purpose of money is leverage – to buy the things we want and need. In reality, whoever has more money typically calls the shots.

Our conditioning about money is what shapes our attitudes and ideas about these specific pieces of paper or metal. We assign values to money that equate with qualities which are subjective and therefore different for everyone. We do this collectively through our cultural desires driven by tradition, and privately, through our families and friends, which help us balance against the overriding saturation of advertising. This is where the problems begin. When we marry, we have expectations about the qualities, values and money styles that may conflict with those of our husband.

Theoretically, it ought to be as easy to talk about money as it is to talk about anything else with our husband. In fact, sex is easier to discuss than money, even though both of these subjects will be a central part of your marriage.

It seems our culture is more supportive of discussions about sex than about money. Everything about sex is more open these days, and there is lots of support for people who need help with sexual problems. Women typically aren't virgins coming into marriage anymore and speak more freely about their needs and desires. We've been, so to speak, 'tested in the field' and not new to sex, which used to be a mystery going into marriage. We go into marriage believing that we are entitled to a good sex life. Our husband also wants to discuss sex because it's important to him to feel that we are sexually satisfied.

Studies show that it's money, not sex, that leads to most marital difficulties and that money issues symbolize deeper concerns like trust, love, security and expectations.

Here's where the reluctance to discuss money gets women in trouble. Even though the law in community property states makes a wife an equal financial partner in her marriage, too many wives either don't know that or don't exercise their right to have access to all the financial information that affects what is called "the community," meaning the financial transactions that are conducted with community property funds.

If money is a loaded topic, as it is for so many women, then there's never going to be an ideal time to talk about it. If you know from experience that it's a hot button subject for your husband as well, that makes it even more important to talk about.

"Cathy," the cartoon by Cathy Guisewite, often hits the nail right on the head. In one of them, Cathy is talking with her CPA:

Cathy: My fiancée and I will never have money problems because we share the same values.

CPA: You have similar savings plans?

Cathy: Um…I don't really know.

CPA: Similar investment strategies?

Cathy: Don't really know.

CPA: Similar spending priorities? Similar diversification goals for your IRA funds?

Cathy: Um…um..

CPA: Which values do you share?

Cathy: We both value how peaceful it is when no one brings up the unpleasant subjects of saving, investing, spending and IRAs!

Imagine yourself having the following conversation before your wedding. Say you've tried to talk about money before and something has always come up to shut the conversation down. You told yourself it was fine even though it really wasn't, and just got busy with other things. After all, there are so many wedding details to take care of and you just know it's going to be fine.

You: "Honey, you know with all the wedding planning and running around, I sometimes forget to tell you how much I love you. "

He: "I love you, too."

You: "I know you do. Hey, you know what I was thinking?"

He: "What?"

You: "That it's good we can talk openly about things that other couples have trouble with. But it dawned on me that there's one subject we haven't really discussed."

He: "What's that?"

You: "Money. We haven't talked about it much and it's important to me."

He: "We did talk about it, honey. Lots of times. We agree we'd get around to the details after we get back from our honeymoon."

You: "Yes, but I think we should talk about it before."

He: "Why? Don't you trust me?"

If you're feeling at all uncomfortable about this conversation, you have every right to be. Communication about money isn't about trust. It's about participation, responsibility and equality in making financial decisions. It's about setting the communication tone. It's about self-esteem and being treated as an adult. It's about financial transparency in this partnership called marriage. It's about safety for you if something happens to your husband. Most of all, it's about intimacy.

While you're dating, you probably got some sense of how compatible your money styles are. The time to talk about money is before you are engaged. By that time, you probably have a clearer sense of how your money styles match up. Furthermore, if there are things that bother you now, they won't go away.

And it's not going to get any easier for you. Your fiancée can't read your mind. He won't know that these things, whatever they are, bother you and will have no reason to change if you remain silent. Once you are engaged, you should feel comfortable enough about most subjects to discuss them with your future husband. At this point, you're moving into a major financial commitment including that big tab for your wedding.

But before your fiancée even comes into the picture, spend some time thinking about the following questions about yourself. Be honest. There is nothing right or wrong about feelings. Understanding why you're feeling the way you are is not something I can cover in this book except in a cursory way. But the questions will provide a framework in which you and your fiancée can begin to talk about money and what it means to each of you.

Remember that financial profile you took a few pages back? Ask your fiancée to fill out the same information. See how willing he is to do that. He doesn't have to share it with you right up front, but his willingness to fill it out will tell you a lot about his initial response to money. If he's willing to share it right away, that's a sign that your future husband will be open to discussing money with you.

It's About More than Money

The questions that follow are not exhaustive, but they will give you points of departure for a deeper discussion. The questions work equally well for when you're talking with your husband (which we will cover in the next section).

I'm sharing my personal answers to some of these questions to show you how deeply ingrained our money attitudes are, even after years of adulthood. These questions deal with four aspects of money and you: memories, assumptions, attitudes, and styles.

Memory

- What is your earliest memory about money?

For example, mine is the time when I was eight years old and I took a quarter out of my mother's purse to buy something she said I couldn't have. She knew I took it because she saw I had the very thing she said I couldn't buy. She scolded me and I remember feeling shame. That early lesson connecting shame with dishonesty has helped to keep me honest. I also dislike situations where people nitpick about small change.

- How was money handled in your family?
- Were your parents generous with it, did they discuss it openly and easily, did they fight about it?
- Did your father use it as leverage with your mother?
- Did she have her own income?
- Did you get an allowance and could you spend it the way you wanted to?
- Were your parents fair about money with your siblings?
- So, what are some of your earliest memories

about money? What feelings come up when you think about them?

- Explore this same question with your fiancée when you're ready.

Assumptions

- What are some of your assumptions about money?

My parents were obsessed with saving money for their old age. In the days before ATMs and the Internet, I remember taking my father's paycheck to the bank for deposit and saying to the teller, "This is for my parents' old age." This little girl would get a laugh every time. I didn't realize until years later that my parents had deprived themselves of a lot of fun and pleasure by postponing things they could have enjoyed years earlier. On the other hand, I never had to help support them in their old age. My assumption about money was that a portion of it should be saved, not necessarily for old age, but set aside on a regular basis. I also vowed not to be like them and have some fun in life before I got old.

Here are a few possibilities:

- Men are better with money than women.
- Because your husband earns more, handling the bills and managing the finances is his job.
- Money equals love; the more expensive the gifts he gives you, the more he loves you.

- Women have no head for numbers and that's why keeping the records is your husband's job.

- I'll stop worrying about money when there is 'enough'.

- What is your definition of 'enough'?

Attitudes

- What about your attitudes about money?

Feelings and attitudes about money are not genetically coded as part of your personality or character. They are learned responses to the attitudes of your family and are closely related to their assumptions about money.

For example, I used to hear that money doesn't grow on trees and that a penny saved is a penny earned. My mother would pick up every penny she saw laying in the street. She would double-check to see if she left any change in the public telephone. I don't do that because I think pennies are a nuisance and should be abolished. But I get a little jolt of guilt when I don't pick up the penny, a little reminder from my youth that money doesn't grow on trees.

You may have heard some of the following:

- Money is the root of all evil. Ever ask yourself why and how that started?

- What about someday our ship will come in? Does that mean to keep trying or to sit back and wait passively for what you want?

- It's a man's job to take care of the finances.

- What about keeping up with the Jones and competition? How will you ever know when you've 'made it'?

- What about equating self-worth with net worth?

- Rich people aren't necessarily happy.

- The best things in life are free.

Your attitudes about money are important to discuss with your fiancée, and to learn about how his own attitudes developed. It's very enlightening to see where the similarities and differences lie.

Styles

Different money styles can become problems if you don't discuss them. For example, I'm comfortable if there is a difference between my bank statement and my check book within $100. If it's less than that, I don't pay attention. If it's more than that, I start rechecking the numbers. This used to drive my husband crazy. He was an engineer and precise about making the numbers match up. We solved it by keeping separate checkbooks, with him keeping the joint checking account that tracked the monthly expenses.

Some other examples of money styles include:

- Do you like to pay bills on time while your mate runs them out until the last day of before the penalty period?

- Are you lavish with gifts while your mate is more conservative?

- What about your willingness to buy retail now while your mate shops around for the best wholesale deal, thereby delaying your home improvement project?

- Do you just sign the credit card slip without paying too much attention to the total, while your mate carefully adds up all the items?

- Do you like to pick up the tab when you go out with friends and have them pick it up next time while your mate insists on settling each person's portion of the bill right there at the restaurant?

By this time, you may be seeing more clearly that money is not just about money. It's about a lot of other issues as well. You can think about it as a blank screen upon which we project a lot of other issues – our fears, and worries and dreams. Or, it can signal a lack of something we're not getting in some other area of our life such as affection, recognition, safety, appreciation, authority, or personal fulfillment.

We often use money to fill the space left by these other areas of unmet needs. For example, is money a mask that hides feelings of dependency, power, mistrust or guilt? Do you use it to test who loves who more?

A few years ago, an ad for a Porsche was submitted to a contest for best ads. It read "Small penis? Have we got a car for you!" Sure it's funny, but it's based on a subliminal fear which many men have about their penis being too small compared to the other guys in the locker room. A powerful Porsche evens the odds outside the locker room. The ad never ran, but those of us who saw it thought it was hilariously effective at getting to the heart of things.

When you've taken the time to think about your own feelings and attitudes about money, and understand yourself a little better, then you're ready to initiate a discussion with your fiancée.

There are two parts to talking about money that you'll find useful. One is more open-ended and falls into the category of general conversation. The second is more focused and concentrates on guidelines for specific areas to explore about your attitudes.

Four steps to take to get the conversation going:

1. Start the dialogue.

Get his attention by telling him you love, admire, value his opinion -- whatever works for your man. Be honest about how important it is to you to be able to discuss money without feeling awkward or defensive, and that you need all the practice you can get. Besides, you don't want anything to interfere with your ability to be intimate with each other.

What does money represent for you on an emotional level? For example, security, self-esteem, independence, validation -- whatever feelings you can identify that link with money. This is an area of brainstorming between the two of you. Remember, there's nothing inherently more special or awkward talking about money than there is about sex. If you need to ask some questions to get the conversation going, try:

How did your family handle money issues?

Were they secretive?

Did your parents argue about it?

Were they generous about money or frugal?

2. Make "I" statements:

- My family was funny about money
- I've tried hard to understand my attitudes about money
- I don't want to repeat their scenario.
- I feel really uneasy when I have no savings.
- Confide your worries, even if you think they're irrational.
- Share your goals and dreams about your future together.

3. Give him time to respond.

Make sure your fiancée has the space and time to respond to what you said and share his own feelings on the subject. Don't rush him, or finish his sentences. He's trying to express himself in his own way.

Don't interrupt or criticize him in any way. They're his feelings, not yours. Think how comfortable he will feel knowing that he can express himself without you interrupting or acting defensive.

Then, take turns discussing what you learned about each other's attitude about money. Share what you're afraid of and also what you admire about his money attitude. If you can't find something to say that will make him feel good, chances are money is going to be a huge issue in your marriage.

4. Reinforce the positive

This may be the most important part of the discussion. Reinforce the admire part. Right from the beginning, you'll be demonstrating to your fiancée that his point of view is as valid as yours. Show him that you intend to listen respectfully and not force his feelings and opinions into your framework. It's easier to get cooperation when someone is being acknowledged in a loving, supportive and non- threatening way.

Discuss the subject in small chunks. Don't devote an afternoon to cover everything. Once you both get comfortable discussing money, it will come up naturally in conversation over the course of time.

Should You Have a Premarital Agreement?

Premarital agreements (or prenuptial agreements) are not new. In fact, they date back to the Babylonians in the first millennium BC. They have always been widely used by royals and the very rich to preserve their fortunes and protect their dynasties.

What is new is the number of 'ordinary' people who want to protect assets each may have acquired before they marry. Some may want to protect inheritances for children from earlier marriages. The premarital agreement defines and resolves issues relating to money, property, prior financial commitments and inheritance. It certainly is a great way for you to get accustomed to talking with your future husband about money.

Think of it this way. A marriage license confers official sanction by the state for you to get married. A premarital agreement is an economic contract between you and your spouse that defines what would happen if your marriage ends, either through death or divorce. The laws regarding premarital agreements vary from state to state and the rules are constantly changing.

If you and your future husband decide to move forward with an agreement, an attorney must draw it up. It should be reviewed by another attorney to assure that both of your interests are clearly defined and represented. Both of you must sign it; it activates only when you marry. Many states require that the agreement must be notarized to be valid. You need professional advice on this, so don't think in terms of anything other than a legal agreement if you want it to be binding.

Before you and your future husband consult a lawyer, you need to be able to discuss the details of what will be included in the document. That's why it's so important that you be able to talk about money before you marry. You may decide after discussion not to have a premarital agreement; many couples choose not to. Either way, being able to discuss it is key to your continuing ability to talk easily and comfortably about money after you marry.

Is a premarital agreement right for you?

Technically, no one needs a premarital agreement. It is usually something one or both parties want or are pressured into by their families, friends, or lawyer. This is an agreement made between perceived un-equals, either in existing assets or anticipated future gains, needs or rights.

There are many reasons you might want a premarital agreement. It could be a desire to keep valuables such as real estate, securities, jewelry, furniture or collectibles as separate property. It could be a desire to clarify obligations to a former spouse, a child from a previous marriage or to your parents. You might want to keep your new spouse from inheriting any part of an existing family business, or cap the level of financial support in the event of a divorce.

Ultimately, a premarital agreement serves as a plan for the end of a marriage, not for how the marriage will be conducted. Like an insurance policy, which you're glad you have if you need it, a premarital agreement doesn't come into play until the end of the game. Unlike an insurance policy, however, a premarital agreement often strikes deep psychological nerves. It can imply a lack of trust or signal that the one who wants the agreement may not believe that the marriage will last and doesn't want to share worldly goods if it ends.

It's true that some couples have postponed weddings indefinitely or broken up after beginning discussions about a premarital agreement. However, that might not be a bad thing. If you can't make it through negotiating a premarital agreement, how can you struggle through the financial discussions that arise as a part of daily life once you're married?

It's important to understand what rights you are giving up when you sign a premarital agreement. Depending on the terms of the agreement, and the laws of your state (these vary from state to state and you should be familiar with these before moving forward), you may be giving up:

- Your right to inherit property upon your husband's death. You may also lose your elective share (the minimum amount of assets your husband must leave to you by virtue of having been married).

- Your right to a fair distribution of assets (or equal division of property in community property states) if your marriage ends in divorce. You may also lose other rights to which you are entitled (they vary by state), such as the right to receive support if you are divorced.

If you're the one asking for an agreement, your husband is giving up the same rights to your assets.

Moving Forward with a Premarital Agreement

Premarital agreements are negotiated and signed before the wedding, a time when most couples are under the stress of planning a wedding as well as the time when they are supposed to be most in love. In first marriages especially, people don't think about the marriage ending. What's really valuable about discussing a premarital agreement is that it gives you a very clear look at how you and your future husband will deal with the subject of money.

Janice, a friend of mine who was marrying for the first time, signed an agreement against the advice of her own attorney. When the marriage ended, the agreement turned out to be a financial disaster for her. She recalls with great bitterness "I didn't want to seem petty or greedy. We were so in love I couldn't imagine it ever ending." Her agreement called for giving up all rights to income and acquired property. "I will always be angry about it – at him, at myself, and at my naiveté."

Vicky, another woman I know, is still married and angry about signing the premarital agreement ten years ago. She admitted that she signed because all the wedding arrangements had been made. "It was embarrassing to call it off," she said. " Friends had made travel plans to attend. We incurred costs up front. When Tom presented me with the request for an agreement, I probably had enough time to think about it, but I didn't want to disappoint my parents and friends."

Vicky now feels trapped and frightened about asserting herself in the marriage because she doesn't want to provoke her husband. "He's holding all the cards," she said. "What's so maddening is that we live in a community property state. The agreement cancels all the protections I would have had."

If you decide to move forward with a premarital agreement, remember a few things required for your agreement to be valid.

A premarital agreement must:

- Be entered into freely and voluntarily.
- It must be in writing and signed by both you

and your future husband before the wedding.

- Both of you must have disclosed all your assets, income and debt.

- Both of you must have had ample time to consider the contents, and must get separate legal advice before signing.

- The agreement must not be fraudulent or signed under duress.

The primary intent of a premarital agreement is to cover what happens in the event of divorce, not death. Yet a premarital agreement is often drawn up to help minimize tension between a new stepparent and adult children who may fear the stepparent will receive their parent's assets upon death.

Remember, a premarital agreement is not a substitute for a will. A will can be signed and changed only by the person who wrote it. A premarital agreement requires change by both parties. You should definitely consult a lawyer if you are marrying someone with adult children to find out how to best protect your financial interests going into marriage.

What should you include in your agreement?

Before you consult a lawyer, you and your husband-to-be should separately prepare the items you want to include. After discussing what you've listed, you may decide to hold some property jointly instead of in separate names. Whatever your major concerns are, you should discuss them with each other before meeting with your respective lawyers.

The following issues are typically covered in a

premarital agreement. However, agreements can be as detailed or broad as you like.

- Prior marital history and family circumstances (children/dependents)

- What property and prospects each of you brings into the marriage

- Who will own the investment earnings from such property

- What will happen with the earnings of husband and wife

- What happens with the property one spouse may inherit

- What happens in the event of the death of one spouse

- Where you will live

- How taxes will be filed (i.e. joint or separate returns)

- The level of support in the event of a divorce

- What happens to debts owed before the marriage and those incurred afterward

- Does a life insurance beneficiary need to be changed? Is the level of coverage adequate for your new family?

- Does either party have aging parents who are dependent now or may become so? Will they live with you? Who will care for them? What financial help will be given?

- Formal periodic reviews of the premarital agreement. If modifications are required, agree for each party to seek separate legal counsel.

Summing up

A premarital agreement can create an atmosphere of open discussion before you marry. This will carry over so that future concerns about money, work, children, the home and other mutual issues can be freely discussed. The clause in the agreement that allows for modification of the contract is very important. This provision allows for flexibility in coping with changed circumstances such as the birth of a child, changing professions, or the passage of a certain amount of time.

If you do make changes, follow the same procedure you used when you drew up the original document. Check if your state requires that the document be notarized. State clearly whether you're replacing the previous document or simply changing certain terms in the previous one.

Chapter Thirteen

* * *

Money Talk After Marriage

Love does not consist in gazing at each other,
but in looking together in the same direction.

Antoine De Saint-Exupery

B eginning to talk about money after you've been married for five, ten, or more years may seem like a daunting task. Let's say your husband has been handling the finances all those years. How do you suddenly begin to talk about participating? Your husband may get angry when you raise the subject. He may be resistant to sharing information with you. Why, after so many years of letting him do things his way, do you suddenly want to know about the finances? Don't you trust him? Are you planning divorce? Will you be buying something big without telling him?

How do you raise the subject of planning and money and your concern about being widowed? How do you encourage your husband to face his mortality? How do you keep him from feeling threatened if he's always handled the finances and now you're trying to 'invade his territory'?

On the other hand, let's assume the best case scenario. Your husband wants you to know about the finances. He's been trying for years to get you to take a more active role. You weren't interested. You were 'too busy.' Whatever your excuse has been up to now, you're going to change that. Now you're not only asking for information, but you're asking him to plan with you.

If you're one of the lucky women whose husband wants you to get involved in the finances, you're way ahead of the game. However, your husband may still be reluctant to discuss the possibility of his death. He may be open and generous with financial information, but resistant to planning. He may be superstitious and think that planning causes people to die sooner. He may feel as if God is watching who plans and who doesn't and decides that the good planners have to go first.

So even when you get the financial information, you still need for him to be open to your desire to plan and consult an estate attorney with you. Remember, your objective is to translate his desire to protect you into concrete action. Intending to do so isn't enough. Nothing is legal until it's written out in detail, signed and dated.

How will you get this process started? More importantly, how will you stay on track until you get the results you want and need?

———————

In the seminar I present, we role play a game called "The Cigar and the Rose." We break into couples. Two women play a couple. The women holding the rose play the wife. The ones holding the cigar are the husband. After the first round of the conversation below, they switch roles.

Rose: "I'm worried because I don't understand our finances."

Cigar: "Don't worry. It's all taken care of."

Rose: "I know, but I would feel safer if I knew what was going on."

Cigar: "Have I ever let you down?"

Rose: "No, but what if something happens to you?"

Cigar: "Nothing is going to happen to me."

Rose: "But unexpected things happen to people all the time."

Cigar: "There you go, nagging me again."

The goal is to keep the dialogue going beyond the gridlock caused by the last sentence. Many women are surprised by how differently they feel when they are holding the cigar. They express themselves more forcefully and directly than when they are holding the rose.

"With the cigar, I feel strong and powerful. It's easy for me to shut the rose down," said Abby, one of the participants. "When we switch, and I am the rose, I back off just like I do at home."

How can a symbol, a cigar or a rose, make such a difference in how we speak and act? Why can a cigar make us feel assertive, firm and powerful while holding a rose makes our voice softer, our words more tentative and our body language more submissive?

Abby is one of dozens of women who have asked if they could have a cigar to take home with them. I go through a lot of cigars in the course of a year! No one has ever asked for a rose.

As you read the following chapters, remember a few things:

Visualize yourself with a cigar, and not a rose. Remember your two-fold objective – to get the financial information that affects you and to get your husband to take action with you.

Be aware that a resistant husband requires more patience and creativity than one who has been waiting to share information with you. You may be uncomfortable doing what I suggest. You may feel manipulative or deceptive. You may feel angry that you're in this situation in the first place. It's normal, and you'll move past it if you keep your eye on your objective. It's worth it. The feeling of warmth, trust and intimacy you will achieve when you realize how willing your husband is to share information with you will surprise you.

———————————

The keys to communicating effectively about the subjects of money and death are timing and location, your tone, the content of your discussion, and your intention to follow through.

Timing and Location

Remember we said earlier that there is never a good time to raise the subject? Not only is this true, but there are actually some particularly bad times. Is your husband looking forward to the Sunday afternoon football or soccer game on television? Has he had a bad day at the office? Are your parents coming to visit? Has he been looking forward to the weekend to go sailing with his buddy from out of town?

It doesn't matter what it is. What matters is that his attention is on something that's important to him. It may not necessarily be a good thing that's on his mind, but he'll be preoccupied with it.

At such times, leave him alone. He's not going to react well to your desire for a conversation about finances. I wouldn't, and neither would you. Give him the courtesy of knowing that you have something you want to talk to him about and ask when that would work for him.

He may be surprised that you're even asking to set up a time that's convenient for him. He might ask what it's about. Tell him it's about some things you've been thinking about and you'd value his input. And that it will only take 30 minutes. And that you'll be at the kitchen table.

Why am I suggesting that you make an appointment and set a 30-minute time limit on it? What's so special about the kitchen table? Well, because in the first few minutes of your conversation, your husband will be uncomfortable. Five minutes will seem like an eternity to him. If you set up a timer, he'll see you're serious about the time limit. He'll see that he's not going to be on the hot seat for longer than that. You're bringing up an uncomfortable subject. He will hear it as criticism and judgment and he'll be itching to get away. When that timer goes off, you'll be thanking him for his time, and you'll be making another appointment.

By having this initial conversation at the kitchen table, you're allowing him to respond without being self-conscious as he would be in a public place. The strange thing about uncomfortable feelings is that when we're having them, we think other people can see how we really feel. Most of the time, no one is paying attention to us. But that's not how it feels when we're discussing something uncomfortable. The kitchen table is familiar and neutral. He'll feel he can get away if he needs to.

Don't schedule your appointment close to bedtime. Don't raise the subject at any other time except during your agreed appointment time. You want your man as comfortable as he can be. And you want him to trust you with sticking to your agreement.

Imagine his surprise! You kept your word, you respected his schedule, you asked for his input – and you didn't criticize him for anything. He'll be a lot more relaxed the next time you discuss things.

Maybe you won't have to discuss it again. My husband didn't like to talk about 'our relationship.' We knew we loved each other, so what was the big deal? Early in our marriage, he told me, "Helga, I can't read your mind. If there is a problem, tell me what it is, and tell me what you want me to do about it." I had to learn how to be direct and specific. He was an engineer – logical, practical, and methodical. I am a writer - intuitive, sensitive, and I can find many ways to say something to keep from having to say it directly.

I'm ashamed to admit that even in my forties, I believed that if my husband really loved me, he would know instinctively what I wanted. I also expected, subliminally, childishly, that because I wanted it, he would give it to me.

I am an only child. In my family, people were always aware of 'how the child is feeling.' He was the baby in his family, and he was accustomed to speaking up for what he wanted and needed. So I had to learn to talk with him in language with which he was comfortable.

What surprised me was how easy it eventually became to say "This is the problem and this is what I'd like you to do about it." Once he pointed it out to me, I found it freeing not having to beat around the bush. You don't have to play guessing games. Sometimes, it was the launching point for more discussion; other times, the statement about the problem and solution was enough for him to take care of it.

In the long run, it saved me a lot of time and heartache to be specific about what I wanted or needed. I practiced a lot by rewriting and restating the things that bothered me until I could distill them into a sentence. I didn't always get what I was asking for, but at least there was clear discussion about where our boundaries were and what I had the right to ask for and what was off limits.

I didn't realize, until I was doing the research for the seminar, just how uncomfortable men are with discussions about 'the relationship.' That doesn't mean he doesn't care. It's just that he doesn't like feeling less articulate or expressive than his wife. He assumes that you will tend to the emotional care and feeding of the relationship. Talking about 'the relationship' feels like criticism or judgment to him. So he'd rather not do it. If you have a problem, he wants to know what it is and what you want him to do about it. Then go out and enjoy your favorite restaurant.

Before we get to specific ways to raise and sustain the subjects of money and death, here are some ground rules:

1. Stick to the time limit. That's what the timer is for. Thirty minutes feels like a long time if you're not enjoying the conversation.

2. Treat your husband as if he were just your friend. It's sad but true that we take liberties talking with our husband that we'd never take with our friends. That means don't interrupt, don't be sarcastic, let him finish his own sentences, don't tell him what he means, and don't raise your voice. Any one of these behaviors is counterproductive to what you're trying to achieve in these conversations.

3. Be specific about what you want. Don't generalize about his behavior and don't blame him for anything. If you do, he'll feel shame, and he'll shut you out. The conversation will be over before you begin.

4. Stick to the facts about wanting to participate in the finances and setting up protection in case something happens to him. That's the point of the conversation. Don't bring up emotional baggage you've been carrying around for years.

5. Avoid using phrases like "you always" or "you never" or "you used to" or "you should have."

6. Use sentences that deal with your feelings and take responsibility for them. "I'm concerned" or "I realize" or "I'm frightened" or "I worry."

7. If you disagree, do so politely and fairly by acknowledging his point. Explain why you disagree and ask him to comment on your reason. You're entitled to disagree, but not to shout him down doing it. You might spend your whole time talking about one point of disagreement, but the fact that you're still talking when the timer goes off is a very good sign.

8. Remember your objective. You may be giving the performance of your life the first time you follow these guidelines, but you'll be surprised at how effective they are and how good you will feel about him when he responds.

9. Let him have the last word. When he's finished, thank him for his time and attention (without sarcasm, disdain or drama) and ask when it would be convenient to schedule some more time.

10. Under no circumstances should you mention anything about his mother.

Imagine your husband's response! You kept your word, you respected his schedule, you asked for his input – and you didn't criticize him for anything. He'll be a lot more relaxed when your next appointment rolls around.

Raising the Subject

We've established the guidelines. You're clear on your objective and your appointment is on the calendar. Now we're ready to raise the subject.

Before we do, remember you're not trying to change your husband across the board. That's a subject beyond the scope of this book. You're not necessarily looking for a change in his thinking. What you're after is a change in behavior to protect you financially through planning, making your marital finances transparent, and improving the level of intimacy between you as you learn how to talk with each other.

If discussions have been uncomfortable for your husband in the past, he may be bracing himself for a repeat of whatever he has experienced with you previously. He'll be remembering the discussions that started off quietly and escalated into arguments. Why should this one be different?

Unfortunately, too many of us coast along when things are going the way we want them to and get on his case when there's something we don't like. It's almost Skinnerian in its simplicity.

B.F. Skinner, noted behaviorist in the early 50s, formulated a theory about reinforcing behavior you want to encourage: reward the behavior you like, ignore what you don't like. We seem to do it in reverse fashion. We take the good parts of our relationship for granted, because after all, don't we feel entitled to that? But when our husband does something that we don't like, we roar into action or sulk or withhold sex or give him the silent treatment.

But this conversation will be different. You will be giving your husband what husbands want most and get least -- acknowledgement, appreciation and recognition.

Opening the Dialogue

For starters, thank your husband for setting the time aside to speak about something that's very important to you. Acknowledge that you know there are other things he might rather be doing and that you appreciate his willingness to talk. He'll be able to relax because you're saying things that show you are sensitive to the fact that he is participating even though he may not want to.

Now you're ready to introduce the subject. The important thing to remember is that he doesn't have the objective you have. He may love you very much and still be resistant to talking about his mortality and how that would affect you. You'll no doubt find many examples of your own, but I'll share one of mine that may give you additional perspective:

When I first raised the subject with my husband, he was surprised that I was even worried about being widowed. He told me he never worried about my dying. "We're young, we're healthy, we have decades to look forward to, we're rarely sick, our health profiles are excellent, we're enjoying life. The time we spend talking about this is depressing; we could be planning our next vacation instead of planning for something bad happening to me. Come on, honey, things have never been better. Maybe it's hormonal....and so on. Everything he said was true.

We had three conversations that followed this pattern before he realized how important this was to me. It didn't sink in for him until I pointed out that everything he had built, that we had built together, was at risk because nothing was in writing. I didn't tell him that I was very uncomfortable about his son who had never fully accepted my place in his father's life. I knew that if things were not in writing, I was not only at risk, but surely in danger of losing out after nearly two decades of financial participation in our life together.

There are a few ways to start these conversations. One is the story angle where something happened that reminded you to speak to your husband about your own concerns. These might include:

- "I read about a woman who..."

- "I'm really concerned about..."

- "A friend told me about a woman who..."

- "At the office, they were talking about..."

- "On one of the money talk shows, this woman called in..."

- "If you were me, what would you do about..."

- "Remember ____? Someone said she had to sell her house when her husband died. I'm scared that could happen to me."

The other way to ease into this conversation is by starting with acknowledgement and appreciation:

- "One of the things I've always loved about you is..."

- "I can't imagine life without you because..."

- "I've always appreciated the fact that you..."

- "Over the years, you've always taken care of the finances and I've really appreciated that. But lately, I've been wondering how I would ever manage on my own if something happened to you."

You're the one who knows your husband best, so you can finish the sentence with something personal that makes sense for your relationship. I can't stress enough the importance of respect, kindness, and appreciation as precursors to conversation.

Relearning your ABCs

Albert Ellis was one of the earliest proponents of cognitive therapy, a method frequently used by psychologists to help people deal with issues without spending years in talk therapy. Ellis calls his method rational emotive therapy. It's based on ABC – specifically, it's not what happens at point A that determines how you feel about it at point C. It's what you tell yourself at point B about what happened at Point A that determines how you feel about it at point C.

When you apply the ABC method to conversations, you can minimize defensiveness and allow the other person to hear you better because you're not accusing him of anything. You're taking responsibility for how you respond to certain behavior. Instead of saying "You do this or you do that," if you rephrase it along ABC lines: "When I see (or hear, or think) you do A, I think B and respond C." One way to get comfortable with the ABC format is to try writing it out. For example, "When I don't know about our finances, I think you're trying to shut me out and I feel resentful and insecure." That's a lot different than saying "You don't care about my feelings."

ABC statements begin with "I" ("When I have to nag you for information…") and not "You" ("When you won't tell me what's going on…"). Comments that begin with "You" automatically promote defensiveness.

How many times will you have to have these conversations? I don't know because we all have a different relationship. But if you're going to need more than one conversation, review the guidelines, schedule another appointment and do it again.

The Case for Postmarital Agreements

While a premarital agreement may date back many centuries, a postmarital agreement is relatively new. It is a voluntary contract between a husband and wife. created after the wedding in the context of a continuing and viable marriage. This form of marriage contract is rapidly gaining in popularity. Marriage counselors and lawyers frequently encourage the discussion of a postmarital agreement to help promote harmony in troubled marriages. The reasoning is that the process of discussion can be a positive influence on the dynamics between husband and wife.

Postmarital agreements often serve the same purpose as premarital ones. However, courts scrutinize them more carefully, often holding them to a higher standard of fairness because both parties have less leverage after they marry than before.

Unlike premarital agreements, there is no uniform law that applies to postmarital ones. Their validity varies from state to state. However, the same basic rules apply for all marriage contracts. They must be drawn up by a lawyer, each party must have separate legal counsel, they must be valid in the state in which you live, they cannot have been created under duress and they must accurately disclose and reflect the full financial situation between you and your husband.

Things to Consider

It's never too late to assess, define and protect your own participation in a partnership. You might not have had a premarital agreement, or perhaps you aren't comfortable with what it says. Your life situation may be different: a career change, becoming a parent or taking care of one, an inheritance, a disability, an entrepreneurial venture or any other financial change could occur. Creating a postmarital agreement might make you feel emotionally and financially safer.

Unlike a premarital agreement, the purpose of a postmarital one is not primarily to protect against divorce, but to clarify issues within the context of an ongoing marriage.

Remember, a postmarital agreement does not replace a will. The agreement is between you and your husband. A will is a guideline for you and the state. You and your husband should each have your own will. A postmarital agreement will apply to both of you.

Items for Consideration

- Your separate and community assets and debts as well as future income expectations.

- Your spending habits, roles and responsibilities and any concerns you have over money matters.

- Your assumptions and expectations of how property would be handled in the case of death or divorce.

- The agreement must be drawn up with legal help. Each of you should have separate counsel.

- Review the contract periodically, especially if your lifestyle or financial status changes drastically.

- If you move to a different state, check to make sure the laws or legal precedents don't affect the status of your contract.

Remember: With the information and tools you now have in talking about money, it will be easier for you to raise the subject and discuss it calmly.

What should you include in a postmarital agreement?

1. All assets, liabilities, income, and expectations of gifts and inheritances.

2. A description of how debts will be paid

3. What happens to your post-marital property

with regard to appreciation, gains, income, rentals, dividends and proceeds of such property in the event of death or divorce.

4. What happens to your postmarital property in the event of death or divorce.

5. Who will own the marital residence and secondary home in the event of death or divorce.

6. The status of gifts, inheritances, and trusts either spouse receives or benefits from, whether before or after marriage.

7. Medical, disability, life insurance or long-term-care insurance coverage. Who will pay for these?

8. Detail death benefits, stating what you will provide for in your will.

9. Figure out alimony, maintenance, or spousal support, or provide for a waiver or property settlement instead of support (to the extent allowable by law).

Raising the subject of a postmarital agreement can be a sensitive subject, especially if your husband's reaction is to view it as a sign that you are considering divorce. It is obviously easier to bring up the topic if you already have a premarital agreement in place, since the postmarital is just a natural extension of that document.

However, if you haven't discussed marriage contracts before, review the information in the previous chapter dealing with talking about money.

Review the importance of timing, location and tone. Remember the prefaces about appreciation, recognition, acknowledgment and support. Approaching the topic from a collaborative viewpoint is crucial.

For example, if you are a stay at home parent, focus on the need to address your respective contributions to the relationship. State your concerns in a straightforward fashion. Be sure to solicit your husband's input and feedback. Stay open-minded and be prepared to make compromises in the discussion.

Remember your ABCs

At the end of the previous chapter, we noted briefly the value of ABC statements. These begin with an "I" and not a "You". Therefore, when you begin the discussion, you'll be opening with an "I" statement that deals with what you think or feel about a situation.

Here are some discussion starters:

"Now that I've quit my job to be a stay-at-home mom, I feel that we need to discuss my contribution or worth in the relationship."

"Mom is talking about my inheriting the family business. I'm concerned about what would happen in the case of death or even divorce. I need to be confident that the business stays in the family."

"It's been awhile since we have discussed the financial status of our relationship. Can we set aside some time to really talk about money matters and discuss the option of creating a marriage agreement?"

"I'm really uncomfortable about some of the issues we didn't address in our prenup. I'd really appreciate it if we could talk about it and our changed situation today."

Once again, you know your husband best so you can tailor these comments to suit your individual situation. Once again, I can't stress enough the importance of respect, kindness and appreciation as precursors to any conversation.

Give Him the Flowers Now

Closed eyes can't see the white roses;
Cold hands can't hold them, you know.
Breath that is stilled cannot gather
The odors that sweet from them blow.
Death, with a peace beyond dreaming
Its children of earth doth endow;
Life is the time we can help them;
So give him the flowers now.

Here are the struggles and striving;
Here are the cares and the tears;
Now is the time to be smoothing
The frowns and the furrows and fears.
What, to closed ears, are kind sayings?
What, to hushed heart, is deep vow?
Naught can avail after parting,
So give him the flowers now.

Anonymous

Chapter Fourteen

* * *

Give Him the Flowers Now

"Non, je ne regrette rien."

Edith Piaf

Earlier in the book, you had a chance to imagine how you might feel if you could write your husband a letter after he died. You could say anything you wanted or needed to.

Well, let's take that process a little bit further. Let's imagine he could somehow read your letter. You have to stretch a little further for this one, but let's say you invited him to be as honest in his letter to you as you were to him. What do you suppose are some of the things he might want to say to you?

Now I want you to write yourself a letter – from your husband.

Imagine he has read the letter you wrote him after his death. What will he say to you? Answer these questions from your husband's point of view in your letter:

- What was good about your marriage?

- What could have been better?

- What would he have liked to change if he could have?

- What did you bring to his life that he would not have had without you?

- Why did he fall in love with you and choose to spend his life with you?

- What did he love best about you?

- What drove him nuts?

- What would he like to ask your forgiveness for?

- What was he proudest of in his life?

- What gave him the greatest satisfaction in your life together?

- What is his greatest regret about your life together?

- What would he like to thank you for?

Isn't it strange that you can write these letters from not only your point-of-view, but his as well? You already know, <u>now</u>, while your husband is still alive, what the problems are, what he wants from you, what you want from him. If you take some time to write this letter, I think you'll see your husband differently.

You're the one who knows him best. You're the one he turned to for closeness, for intimacy, for emotional connection, for trust. Over time, the luster of your relationship may have dimmed, but if you can, through honest emotional expression, reconnect with your deepest feelings from when you first married, you'll realize that this is still the man you loved enough to marry.

Whether you share these letters with him is up to you. I asked my husband to take the time to go through the process with me. He did, and I discovered that he was resentful about many things. These included my breaking agreements we had made and taking him for granted in situations where I expected him to bail me out. I even learned that he wanted to have sex more often than we were having it.

He felt unappreciated when I asked for help with a problem, then told him he didn't understand. He hated it when I nagged about something he already said he would do, even though it wasn't on my time schedule. He recoiled every time I asked him to tell me how he was 'really feeling.' And why did I make social plans for us both without asking him if he wanted to go?

The money thing was a big one. He was working as hard as he could to make the company succeed. What did I expect him to do? Bail out, sell the company? Why was I such a crybaby when it came to doing my share?

But I also learned why he fell in love with me, what he respected about me, what I brought to his life and how I let a lot of that fall by the wayside in our years together.

When we compared our letters, we found that our difficulties and differences overlapped. But the things we loved about each other and the values we shared were still strong. Because the foundation of this process is based on imagining that the other person is gone, it gave us a degree of freedom to be honest with each other that we couldn't get to in verbal discussion. After all, we were both theoretically 'dead' at that point.

I credit this process with allowing me to heal with 'clean' grief rather than with the guilt, anger, resentment or regret that I have heard so many other widows express in my interviews with them. If my husband had not died when he did, I believe we could have used what we learned to strengthen our marriage.

Chapter Fifteen

* * *

For Husbands Only

A t this point, you've spent some time working your way through the book and its exercises. The book has likely made its way from the bed stand, to the sofa, to the kitchen counter, maybe even the bathroom!

With this book hanging around so much, I'm sure your husband will soon be asking 'what in the world is that book you've got all over the house,' if he hasn't already!

Consider this your final exercise: have your husband read just this chapter. I think you'll find it will give him a better understanding of not only how you're feeling, but why this process is so necessary for you as his partner and wife.

A Letter to Your Husband
How to Be a Hero

I have a cartoon pasted above my desk showing two men in angel garb, each with a halo, floating on a heavenly cloud. One says with a big smile,

"I love this. I've been up here for 11 years, and my will is still in probate!"

This is a cartoon and, of course, we smile. But in real life, having your will drag on in probate will create heartache, headache and expense for your widow. You might laugh and say, "What do you mean, 'my widow'? I'm not planning on dying any time soon."

Great. I hope you don't, because the best way to protect your wife against widowhood is for you not to die. But eventually, of course, you will, just like the rest of us. We just don't know when that will happen.

U.S. Census statistics show that your wife will outlive you. I agree it's tough to think about, but the average age at which a woman is widowed is 56 years old. Your widow might be on either end of that mean average.

My husband died in an accident. He was in great health and looking forward to all the things he would do when he retired. The company he built was finally on solid ground. His tennis game got better every day. The children were grown, doing well, both dogs were trained, and life was good. He didn't plan on dying, but he was smart enough to know that he wasn't in charge of the timing. I like to think he loved me enough to take me seriously when I shared how worried I was about all the legal and financial details we didn't have in place.

If you're not thinking about how that wonderful woman you're married to will cope without you, I think you underestimate how much you mean to her. If you're not openly sharing the details of your joint financial life and if she doesn't know what your joint net worth is, it's fair to guess that you don't consider her to be an equal partner in your marriage.

The problem is that Uncle Sam does consider her an equal partner, especially if you live in a community property state. By legal and financial definition, your wife takes on half of the financial responsibility in your household. If you die, your widow will have to pay off your creditors, even if she doesn't know about them.

If you don't have a will, a revocable living trust, and a durable power-of-attorney for medical and financial decisions in case you are incapacitated, I think you are showing your wife a side of you that isn't heroic or manly. You're engaging in avoidance behavior, thinking that if you don't pay attention to something negative, it won't happen. The funny thing is, none of us is powerful enough to decide if something will happen to us or when it will happen. The only thing within our control is to plan for the things we can't control.

Your wife, whom you say you love, may never tell you how worried she is about being widowed. She may have tried a few times to raise the subject, but somehow you manage to turn her off by accusing her of nagging or being negative. So she's stuck. She can't write your will for you or create a living trust alone. She can't take your medical exam so you can get an insurance policy. She can't draw up an estate plan if you won't cooperate with her. If you're in denial about your mortality, you're placing the woman you love at risk.

Think of it this way. The woman you married, perhaps many years ago, may still be at your side. But she may not be as trusting or comfortable with you as she used to be. You've changed in her eyes because you're not meeting one of her deepest needs – the need to feel protected and secure in this relationship in which she invested so much love, time, effort and faith over the years. That wonderful woman, without whom you might be lost, is not going to suddenly be able to take charge of the finances if she hasn't been involved before.

You have a chance to do something truly heroic. Bite the bullet. Face your mortality. Be the man who loves his wife enough to provide for her even though you're not there to enjoy it with her. Get long-term care insurance so she doesn't spend her own golden years taking care of you. Share the financial records with her. If she doesn't understand them, explain things to her. Introduce her to your broker, lawyer, and accountant. Urge her to meet with them whenever you do. The questions she asks are not dumb questions; they're merely unanswered questions that clear up with a more thorough explanation.

If you really meant those wedding vows of love, honor and cherish, here's your chance to walk the talk. Life without you will be hard enough for the woman you love. Don't add to her grief and loss by leaving her with a financial burden she may not know how to handle.

Real men face their mortality. That's what makes them heroes.

Part Four

Practicing Safe Marriage

Chapter Sixteen

✳ ✳ ✳

Achieving Financial Intimacy

"The end of man is an action, not a thought."

Thomas Carlyle

N ow it's time for action. The pages that follow contain checklists that tell you what you need to know, to have, and to do. You'll find detailed work sheets in the appendix of the book. Copy these and fill in the information with your husband. Keep your worksheets from year to year. Updating them annually will keep you current on your marital finances.

The last section in this chapter is information about what to do in the case of sudden death. I sincerely hope you never need it , but if you do, you will find it invaluable. When my husband died, my daughters used this guide as a tool to help them create some order over the chaos that engulfed us.

In this chapter, we will cover the following:

1. The Basic Planning Questions

2. Financial Information You Should Know

3. Determining Your Net Worth

4. Documents To Keep Together

5. Choosing a Lawyer

6. What Your Estate Plan Should Include

7. Understanding Your FICO Score

8. What To Do If Death Occurs

1. THE BASIC PLANNING QUESTIONS

- Does your husband have a current will suitable to the size your estate? Was it drawn up by an attorney?

- Does he have a revocable living trust? Are you the successor trustee?

- Do you have signed papers giving you durable power of attorney for health care and durable power of attorney for financial decisions if he is incapacitated?

- Does your husband have life insurance? Are you the beneficiary?

- Is the amount adequate to support your needs?

- Do you know where all your joint income comes from?

- Do you know all your (if you work) and your husband's employee benefits?

- Can you meet continuing monthly expenses with only your income if your husband is disabled, becomes ill or dies?

- Do you understand your joint tax return before you sign it?

- Does your husband own a business? Do you know his business associates?

- Is this business your major source of joint income?

- What kind of continuity has your husband provided for the business?

- Are you in your own business?

- Can you afford to continue it if something happens to your husband?

- Do you know your husband's attorney, accountant and financial consultant?

- Do you have disability insurance?

- Can you continue your health insurance if you were to be widowed or divorced?

- Could you afford to live in your home if something happens to your husband?

- How would you pay for the children's education (if they are under 21)?

- What are your current debts?

- Do you have long-term care insurance?

- Do you know your joint credit rating?

- Have you established credit in your own right?

2. FINANCIAL INFORMATION YOU SHOULD HAVE

Worksheets that allow you to list detailed information are included at the back of the book. This list is an overview of what you need to know.

All insurance coverage

- Names of companies
- Items covered – Life, home, car, medical, personal property)
- Policy numbers
- Amount of coverage for each policy
- Due dates for premium payments
- Beneficiary for each policy

Please note: Whether the insurance payment schedule is monthly, quarterly, or annual, it's imperative that you pay the premium on time. You must know if there is a grace period for payment, and don't go beyond that. If you do, there will be penalties. You even run the risk that the policy will be cancelled. That means you don't have insurance when you think you do!!!

This is one of the biggest dangers with differing money styles. If your husband pays the bills, be sure you keep current about the insurance payments.

Securities (stocks, bonds, mutual funds, munis, T-bills, etc)

- Name and location of broker(s)

- Account numbers for each account
- Kinds and amounts of securities held by broker
- Types and amounts at other locations: safety deposit box, home safe, file cabinet, etc.
- Purchases and sales confirmation slips
- Stock options from husband's employer
- Plan for exercising options while husband is alive; (if husband should die ,terms may change)

Other Investments
- Real Estate, loans, tax shelters, coins, art
- Amounts and terms of investment (interest, mortgage, insurance)
- Pending orders for investments and where placed
- Information on legacies, royalties,etc
- Credit union and pension plans of husband's employer
- Retirement asset accounts (IRAs, Keogh, etc.)
- IOUs – money owed to you and your husband

Know amounts and due dates of:
- All mortgages
- Insurance policy premiums
- When the premiums are due

- Taxes (Income and property)
- Outstanding loans – amounts and maturity date
- Installment payments and interest
- Credit card numbers – yours and his

Husband's Work Information

- Husband's social security number
- Company benefits:

    Life insurance
    Health Insurance
    Pension
    Stock options (if applicable)
    401K

If your husband runs his own business, you need to know:

- Who his associates and advisors are
- Succession plan for business in case he dies, ie., sell, run it, etc.
- Paper work for major agreements or where paperwork is filed

A Few Words About Taxes

Every year on or around April 15, millions of wives are asked by their husbands to sign a joint income tax return. My husband used to say "Sign here Honey" at 9:00 pm on April 15 as he raced into the house with the tax return he'd just picked up from his accountant. I'd sign without giving it a second thought.

But "Sign here Honey" are three words that can come back to haunt you if you are ever divorced or widowed. I didn't understand what I was looking at in the stack of papers I had to sign. A lot of what I didn't understand came back to haunt me after I was widowed.

Whether the return is prepared by your husband or an accountant, once you sign the return, you are attesting that you understand and agree that the information as stated on the return is accurate. However, a closer look at the return might show you that your husband has more income than you thought. You might find an IRA or a KEOGH plan that you didn't know about. Perhaps there is a business partnership you didn't know about.

The law requires that a couple is jointly and individually responsible for paying the correct amount of taxes on the taxable income. If you earn less, you will still be held liable if your husband does not pay the correct amount of taxes and falls into default. What you don't want is to find out after a separation, divorce or death that you owe money for taxes.

How do you learn more? First, ask your husband. He isn't necessarily trying to hide things from you by doing the taxes. He does them because you don't want to or you think it's his job. If he is preparing the return, he might be delighted that you're interested. If an accountant is doing your joint return, attend the meeting with your husband. Ask questions about anything you don't understand. Chances are your husband doesn't understand a lot about the tax return as well. The point is, you have to be involved because if something isn't set up right and it affects you, it's harder to untangle the mess after a separation, divorce or death. Do things right from the start.

3. DETERMINING YOUR NET WORTH

What You Own minus What You Owe = Your Net Worth

These are lists. Detailed worksheets are at the back of the book.

Assets

Personal Property:

- House(s)
- Belongings: Furniture, collections, jewelry
- Vehicles (cars, boat, truck, etc.)

Financial Assets

- Securities (Stocks, bonds, mutual funds,
- Checking/Savings
- CDs, Money Market Accounts

Real Estate

- Business Partnerships
- Stock options and bonuses
- Retirement Funds. (Pension, Keogh, IRAs,)
- Life Insurance (Cash and Benefit value)

- Possible Inheritance/Royalties
- IOUs

Total Estimated Assets

$ _____

Liabilities
Taxes

- Social Security
- Federal
- State
- Property

Loans

- Mortgage
- Business
- Personal
- Vehicle
- Home Equity
- Credit Cards

Total Estimated Liabilities

$ _____

Estimated Net Worth

$ _____

4. DOCUMENTS YOU SHOULD KEEP TOGETHER

- Yours and your husband's will and estate plan (Make sure the will is up to date and valid in your state. Keep copies at home and the original with your lawyer. If you change lawyers, be sure to transfer the documents.)

- Birth Certificate for each child (For Social Security benefits for your children if you were to be widowed)

- Marriage license

- Title papers for house and other property

- Ownership papers for vehicles (registration, pink slip)

- Insurance policies (company, policy #, agent's name and phone number)

- Social security numbers (Yours, your husband's, your children if applicable)

- Military discharge papers (You may be entitled to veteran's benefits if your husband was in the armed forces)

- Naturalization and citizenship documents (if applicable)

- Adoption records

- Contracts and Leases (current and completed installment and maintenance)

- Combination to Safe (If you store papers in a fireproof safe, keep the combination in a separate place that easily accessible to you)

- Funeral instructions (If something happens to your husband, you'll need these right away. Keep them where you have easy access to them)

- Keep cancelled checks for at least three years (An IRS audit would require these checks)

- Keep some cancelled checks and papers forever: house purchase; jewelry appraisal and ownership statements; brokerage statements.

- Tax records and returns for previous 5 years.

- W-2s – his and yours

- Dividend and interest statements.

Keep copies of your important documents in a fire proof safe. You can put the originals in a safety deposit box, as long as you're sure you have access to it if you need it.

5. CHOOSING A LAWYER

It can feel intimidating to talk to a lawyer. I've learned the hard way that if your lawyer can't explain things to you as if you were a smart 14-year-old, you probably should find someone who can. I'm not questioning credentials here. I'm just cautioning you to find someone with whom you can communicate easily because, if your husband dies, your lawyer will be key in helping you maneuver through that first year.

If recommended by a friend, ask why this person

likes the lawyer. It's not enough that someone is a friend or a golf partner. You need a lawyer who is experienced in estate planning.

Once you have lawyer in mind, make sure that he or she meets some basic professional criteria:

- offers a free initial consultation to discuss your needs

- has practiced estate planning law for at least five years

- devotes at least 75% of his or her practice to estate planning

- carries professional liability insurance

- bills clients on a fee-for-service basis, rather than an hourly basis

- has earned state bar certification in the field of estate planning (not all state bars offer such certification)

Most of all, you should be comfortable working with the lawyer because you will depend on this person in the early months if your husband dies.

Before your first meeting:

Prepare a list of questions to take with you. Remember, no question is too silly to ask. You just need to have the question answered. Make sure to include these in your questions:

- What does the lawyer need to see in order to evaluate your situation?

- What are other options?

- How many similar matters have he or she handled?

- What percent of his or her practice is in the area of expertise that you need?

- What problems does the lawyer foresee with your situation?

- How would the lawyer go about handling your situation? What is the process?

- How long will it take to conclude the paperwork?

- How does the lawyer charge for his or her services?

- Would the lawyer handle the case personally or would it be passed on to some other lawyer in the firm?

- If other lawyers or staff may do some of the work, could you meet them also?

If you think you have found the right lawyer, ask for a copy of the lawyer's fee agreement. As with all documents, take some time to make sure that you understand it fully before you sign it. No reputable lawyer will pressure you to accept a fee agreement on the spot.

Before Your Next Meeting:

- Save time and money by organizing information about your assets, liabilities, and title arrangements.

- Go in with a written set of questions.

- Discuss your feelings about providing for various family members. Do this before you are in the lawyer's office so you have some idea of how you want to structure your estate.

Bring a tape recorder with you. It's hard to remember all the things your lawyer says. You'll want to review it again later. (There's no legal reason you can't tape your own legal session. If your lawyer objects, tell him you do it with your doctor too. In stressful situations, it's hard to remember what you need to know.)

6. WHAT YOUR ESTATE PLAN SHOULD COVER

- Revocable Living Trust or other Trust Arrangement
- Funding Instructions for the Trust
- Assignment of Personal Property
- Pour Over Will for Husband
- Pour Over Will for Wife
- Community Property Agreement
- Durable Power of Attorney for Husband's Property
- Durable Power of Attorney for Wife's Property
- Advance Health Care Directive with Living Will and HIPAA* Release for Husband
- Advance Health Care Directive with Living Will and HIPAA* Release for Wife

* Authorization for Release of Health Information

You should be the executor of your husband's estate and the trustee of the trust, whether it is a revocable living trust or an irrevocable marital trust. The latter is often used in second marriages where a spouse is concerned that assets are preserved for children of a first marriage. Husbands often prefer a bank, a lawyer, a relative, or a friend to be the trustee for an irrevocable marital trust.

THERE IS NO LEGAL REASON YOU CANNOT BE THE EXECUTOR OR TRUSTEE OF AN IRREVO-CABLE TRUST. You can hire the professional legal assistance you need for advice. If you have a financial professional manage the assets in the trust, you will pay a percentage ranging from one to three percent of the funds under management. If someone else is appointed as the trustee, you will have to petition that trustee if you need more money to live than the trust is generating in income.

Be sure that the trust is set up to allow you to access principal if the trust is generating less income than you need for your health, maintenance and support. Husbands can make a marital trust quite restrictive with regard to access of principal, thus making it hard for you to meet your own living costs. Restrictive provisions in the trust may make you dependent on an outside trustee, who would distribute money to you based on their subjective assessment of your needs.

Remember: A husband and wife often have conflicting interests when estate planning is conducted concerning their property. You and your husband are the clients of the lawyer who is setting up your estate plan. However, if your husband is paying the bills, he is likely to be setting the tone of the transaction. Once the papers are drawn up, don't sign anything until you get a second opinion. Second opinions make good sense when it comes to medicine. They make good sense here as well. Be sure that you understand what the trusts say. It's worth the money to get that second opinion.

7. YOUR FICO SCORE AND HOW IT AFFECTS YOU

A FICO score is a credit score developed by a company called Fair Isaac & Co. It is a compilation of information gathered by the three credit reporting agencies. Credit scoring is a way of determining the likelihood that credit users will pay their bills. A credit score tries to condense a borrower's credit history into a single number on a scale with a low ranking of 650 to a high of 850. Remember, your husband's FICO score affects you as an individual.

Credit scores analyze and rank a borrower's credit history considering numerous factors such as:

- 35% Payment history: If you're late with paying bills, your score will be negatively affected. The more recent the problem, the lower your score. A 30 to 45-day late payment today is worse than a bankruptcy six years ago.

- 30% Outstanding debt: This evaluates how close you are to your credit limit. Owing a little amount on a few different cards is better than being "almost at your limit" on one.

- 15% Credit History: No credit is almost the same as bad credit. So establish credit accounts in your own name while you are married.

- 20% New credit and kinds of credit: Applying for too much new credit will harm your rating.

Increasing Your Credit Score

- Pay your bills on time. Late payments and collections can have a serious impact on your score.

- Do not apply for credit frequently. Having a large number of inquiries on your credit report can worsen your score.

- Reduce your credit-card balances. If you are "maxed" out on your credit cards, this will affect your credit score negatively.

- If you have limited credit, obtain additional credit. Not having sufficient credit can negatively impact your score.

What if there is an error on your credit report?

If you see an error on your report, report it to the credit bureau. There are three major bureaus:

Equifax – www.equifax.com   1-800-685-1111,
Trans Union – www.transunion.com
1-800-916-8800
Experian - www.experian.com 1-888-397-3742

All have procedures for correcting information promptly.

For more information and to find out how you can get your free FICO score, go to www.myfico.com. You are entitled to one free credit report per year.

8. WHEN DEATH OCCURS

This is the section I hope you will never need. However, if you do, it will prove invaluable for your family. It is a checklist for what to do in the early hours after a death. When my husband died, my daughters followed this list.

Immediate Actions

- A doctor or coroner must declare a person dead and sign a death certificate.

- Get at least 20 embossed copies of the original death certificate. You can get these from the hospital, the health department or the funeral director. Every agency or company you will have to deal with will ask for an original certificate. None will accept a photo copy.

- When family members are ready to have the body taken away, call or have someone else call the funeral director of your choice.

- Arrange for members of the family or friends to take turns answering the door or telephone, keeping a careful record of calls.

- Notify your lawyer, executor of the will and your insurance agent.

- Coordinate the supplying of food for the next few days.

- Decide on the time, place and kind of funeral service.

- Make a list of family, friends, and colleagues to be informed. Decide who will inform them.

- Make lodging arrangements for out-of-town relatives and friends.

- Write obituary for appropriate newspapers. Know whom to ask for this.

- If flowers are not wanted, choose charity or hospital, etc. where gifts may be sent. Include this information in the obituary.

- Designate someone to pick up relatives who come in from out-of-town.

- Take extra home precautions against burglars, especially during funeral service.

- Designate person to track flowers, gifts, and donations for later acknowledgement.

Secondary Actions

If you have followed the guidelines outlined in previous sections, you already have much of the information you need to provide to your lawyer. He or she will start the legal proceedings necessary to move you through the estate settlement process. The steps that follow are some that you may need to undertake on your own.

Your Husband's Employer

- Check to determine if you are entitled to any unpaid salary, accrued vacation pay, unsettled expense accounts or bonuses.

- Check accident and life insurance benefits and method of payment and options

- Check retirement plan benefits.

- Clarify stock option requirements if appropriate.

- Convert medical insurance to COBRA* until you can establish insurance in your own name. Ask the human resources department for guidance. *COBRA is a plan approved by the government that allows for temporary continuation of health coverage at group rates.

Life Insurance

- Notify agent. Be ready to supply an original copy of death certificate.

- Ask about options available in collecting the money (lump sum, monthly payments, conversion into annuity program, etc.) Ideally, you should know all this already.

Social Security

- Benefits are paid for each child until 18 years old – or 21 if a full time student.

- Documents and information you need to have to receive your husband's social security benefits:

- Original Copy of Death Certificate

- His Social Security Number

- Your Birth Certificate

- Your marriage license

Safeguarding your Business Interests

- Be sure all accounts have been transferred to your name:
    - Deed of house
    - Stocks and bonds
    - Bank accounts
    - Pay mortgages, leases, income and property taxes and loans on time.

- Don't rush into any investments.

- Put life insurance payment into a money market fund until you can think clearly.

- If a business is involved, see that it continues to operate.

- Don't make any decisions (unless necessary) until you are feeling more emotionally stable.

Selected Bibliography

This selection includes the sources referred to in the text, as well as books and articles that, although not cited explicitly, were useful to my research.

Armstrong, Alexandra & Donahue, Mary R
On Your Own – A Widow's Passage to Emotional and Financial Well Being
Dearborn Financial Publishing, 1993

Esther M. Berger, CFP,
"Money Smart", Secrets Women Need to Know About Money,
Simon & Schuster, 1993

Condon, Gerald M. and Condon, Jeffrey L
Beyond the Grave
HarperBusiness, 1995

Cott, Nancy F.
Public Vows, A History of Marriage and the Nation,
Harvard University Press, 2000

Dowling, Colette
Maxing Out: Why Women Sabotage Their Financial Security
Little Brown & Co., 1998

Farrell, Warren
Women Can't Hear What Men Don't Say
Jeremy P. Tarcher, 2000

Goleman, Daniel
Vital Lies, Simple Truths: The Psychology of Self-Deception
Simon and Schuster, 1985

Graff, E. J.,
What is Marriage For?
Beacon Press, 1999

Hannon, Kerry
Suddenly Single
John Wiley & Sons, Inc., 1998

Johnson, Robert A
We: Understanding the Psychology of Romantic Love
Harper/Collins, 1993

Koontz, Stephanie
Marriage, a History
Penguin Group, 2005

Kushner, Harold S.
When Bad Things Happen to Good People
Avon, 1981

Millman, Marcia
Warm Hearts and Cold Cash: The Intimate Dynamics of Families and Money
Free Press, 1991

Opdyke, Jeff D.
Love and Money
John Wiley & Sons Inc., 2004

Orman, Suze
The Road to Wealth
Riverhead Books, 2001

Quinn, Jane Bryant
Making the Most of Your Money
Simon & Schuster, 1991

Seligman, Martin, E.P. Phd.
Learned Optimism
Alfred A. Knopf, 1991

Viorst, Judith
Necessary Losses
Fawcett Gold Medal, 1986

Additional Resources

General non-technical information about marriage, divorce, financial advice, widowhood:

www.equalityinmarriage.org

www.suzeorman.com

www.ivillage.com

www.biz.yahoo.com

www.smartdivorce.com

www.wife.org

www.smartmarriage.com

Legal Information

www.romingerlegal.com/natbar
(a listing of the 50 state American Bar Associations)

www.nolo.com - legal books for the layman

Appendix

Financial Worksheets For Review and Updating

Copy these and save after you fill them out. By revisiting them in subsequent years, you'll get a clearer view of your marital finances.

Date_____

Insurance

Life:

Coverage _____

Company _____

Policy # _____

Beneficiary _____

Premium _____

Date Due _____

Home:

Coverage _____

Company _____

Policy # _____

Premium _____

Date Due _____

Medical:

Coverage _____

Company _____

Policy # _____

Premium _____

Date Due _____

Personal property:

Coverage _____

Company _____

Policy # _____

Premium _____

Date Due _____

Securities (stocks, bonds, mutual funds, munis, T-bills, etc)

Name and location of broker(s):

(Many men have more than one broker. Be sure you know them all.)

_____

_____

_____

Account numbers for each account:

(Each account has its own identifying number.)

_____

_____

Values and types of securities held by each broker:

(Are they stocks, bonds, mutual funds, treasury notes, money market accounts, municipals, etc.)

_____

_____

Pending orders for securities and where placed:

(special instructions regarding terms of buying or selling stocks and which broker is involved)

_____

_____

Value of stocks or bonds held at locations outside brokerage house:

(safety deposit box, home safe, file cabinet, etc.)

_____

_____

Other Assets

Receipts and sales confirmation slips

(for large purchases, i.e. jewelry, art, boat, etc)

_____

_____

Plan for exercising stock options from husband's employer:

While husband is alive   _____

_____

_____

If husband should die (terms may change)

_____

_____

Pension plan of husband's employer:

Who is beneficiary? At what age is it valid?

_____

Is it fully vested?

_____

Social Security benefits:

You can request a Social Security Statement by visiting their website at http://www.ssa.gov/mystatement, calling 1-800-772-1213, or contacting a local Social Security office. If you visit the website, click on the Benefit Planners tab to get help in planning for retirement. You'll be able to estimate your benefits based on different assumptions about your future earnings or when you plan to stop working.

_____

Retirement asset accounts (IRA, Keogh, etc.):

How are they invested? Have you used any money from these funds?

_____

_____

Real Estate:

Amount of mortgages, equity to date, market value _____

_____

_____

Art:

(appraised value of antiques, coins, paintings, jewelry, etc.)

_____

_____

_____

_____

IOUs – money owed to you and your husband:

(Loans to family members, yours or your husband's business, investment in a friend's company. These should be secured by a note.)

_____

_____

Liabilities

All mortgages:

(Total loan, amount and due date, grace period and penalty for late payment)

_____

_____

Insurance policies:

(The payment – monthly, quarterly, or annual, the amount and due date, the penalty for late payment. Very important because if you are late and the policy is cancelled, you don't have insurance!!!)

_____

_____

Taxes:

(Income, property, business, land – anything for which you receive a tax bill)

_____

_____

Outstanding loans:

(Bank, car, boat, credit cards, etc. Installment amount, due date, grace period for late payment)

Remember: In a community property state, you are responsible for one half of the liabilities if they were purchased with community property funds.

_____

_____

Your Husband's Business

If your husband runs his own business, make sure you know the answers to the following questions:

Who are his associates and advisors?

_____

_____

Is there a succession plan in case he dies, i.e. to sell, run it, etc.?

_____

_____

Have the plans been drawn up?

_____

_____

Where are the documents for these plans?

_____

_____

Is this part of your estate plan?

_____

_____

In a community property state, you are responsible for his business debts, even if the business is incorporated. Find out whether he has signed some of your joint or commingled assets as collateral for the business.

If your husband is not self-employed, make sure you have the company's name written down correctly. Also, be sure to know the name and contact information for you husband's immediate supervisor.

_____

_____

Your Financial Profile

What You Own minus What You Owe = Your Net Worth

Assets:

Personal Property:

House(s):

$ _____

_____

Belongings:

Furniture, collections, jewelry:

$ _____

_____

Vehicles (cars, boat, truck, etc.):

$ _____

_____

Financial Assets:

Securities (Stocks, bonds, mutual funds, etc):

$ _____

_____

Checking Accounts:

$ _____

_____

_____

_____

Savings Accounts:

$ _____

_____

_____

_____

Money Market Funds:

$ _____

_____

CDs:

$ _____

_____

Real Estate:

$ _____

_____

Business Partnerships

$ _____

Stock options and bonuses

$ _____

_____

Retirement Funds (e.g. Pension, Keogh, IRAs, etc.):

$ _____

_____

Insurance (Cash and Benefit value):

$ _____

_____

Deferred Compensation (royalties, bonuses, etc.):

$ _____

_____

Total Estimated Assets

$ _____

_____

Liabilities

Social Security:

$ _____

_____

Current Taxes:

Federal, State & Local:

$ _____

Property:

$ _____

Mortgage/Loans

Residence:

$ _____

_____

Business:

$ _____

_____

Personal:

$ _____

_____

Vehicle:

$ _____

_____

Home Equity:

$ _____

_____

Credit Cards:

$ _____

_____

Stocks on Margin:

$ _____

_____

Total Estimated Liabilities

$ _____

Calculate estimated net worth below.

Estimated Net Worth

(Total Estimated Assets Minus Total Estimated
Liabilities)

$ _____

About the Author

Helga Hayse

Two years before she was widowed in the late 90s, Helga created the seminar "A Wife's Guide to Financial Intimacy" to teach women about the importance of financial participation in their marriage.

She is the founder of The Institute for VitalAging and served as a consultant to business about the growing boomer and senior population.

Helga has presented seminars for New York Life Insurance Company, Merrill Lynch, Allstate Life Insurance Company and a host of community venues. She conducts monthly public seminars for women and private seminars for professional, corporate and community groups.

To learn more about the seminars or order additional copies of the book, visit financialintimacy.com. You can contact Helga directly from the website or call her at 650-345-9294.

I'm currently working on the next book detailing success stories of women who have incorporated financial intimacy into their life and marriage. All personal information is confidential and every effort is made to protect the privacy of individuals.

I would love to hear from you and invite you to contribute the insight you've gained after reading this book and how you applied what you learned.

To submit your story, please contact me at helga@financialintimacy.com.
Or mail your story to,
Financial Intimacy, 205 De Anza, #118, San Mateo, Ca, 94402.

Helga

A Valuable Gift For Every Woman in Your Life

For additional copies of this book:

Online : www.financialintimacy.com

FAX (Send this form): 650-372-9374

Email: helga@financialintimacy.com

Telephone: 650-345-9294.
Have your credit card information ready.

By mail:
Financial Intimacy
205 De Anza, #118, San Mateo, California 94402

Cost: $14.99 (CA residents add 8.25% sales tax)
Shipping and Handling
$4.50 for first book; $2.00 each additional book

Bill to:
NAME :_____
ADDRESS: _____
CITY_____STATE_____ZIP_____
Email:_____
Telephone:_____

Payment: Credit Card
            ❏ Visa   ❏ Mastercard
Card number:_____
Name on card:_____ Exp. date:_____

Ship To:
If different from above:

NAME:_____
ADDRESS:_____
CITY_____STATE_____ZIP_____